Blockchain

Blueprint for a New Economy

Melanie Swan

Beijing · Cambridge · Farnham · Köln · Sebastopol · Tokyo

Blockchain

by Melanie Swan

Printed in the United States of America.

Published by O'Reilly Media, Inc., 1005 Gravenstein Highway North, Sebastopol, CA 95472.

O'Reilly books may be purchased for educational, business, or sales promotional use. Online editions are also available for most titles (*http://safaribooksonline.com*). For more information, contact our corporate/institutional sales department: 800-998-9938 or *corporate@oreilly.com*.

Editor: Tim McGovern
Production Editor: Matthew Hacker
Copyeditor: Rachel Monaghan
Proofreader: Bob Russell, Octal Publishing, Inc.

Indexer: Wendy Catalano
Interior Designer: David Futato
Cover Designer: Ellie Volckhausen
Illustrator: Rebecca Demarest

February 2015:   First Edition

Revision History for the First Edition
2015-01-22:   First Release

See *http://oreilly.com/catalog/errata.csp?isbn=9781491920497* for release details.

978-1-491-92049-7

[LSI]

Table of Contents

Preface

We should think about the blockchain as another class of thing like the Internet—a comprehensive information technology with tiered technical levels and multiple classes of applications for any form of asset registry, inventory, and exchange, including every area of finance, economics, and money; hard assets (physical property, homes, cars); and intangible assets (votes, ideas, reputation, intention, health data, information, etc.). But the blockchain concept is even more; it is a new organizing paradigm for the discovery, valuation, and transfer of all quanta (discrete units) of anything, and potentially for the coordination of all human activity at a much larger scale than has been possible before.

We may be at the dawn of a new revolution. This revolution started with a new fringe economy on the Internet, an alternative currency called Bitcoin that was issued and backed not by a central authority, but by automated consensus among networked users. Its true uniqueness, however, lay in the fact that it did not require the users to trust each other. Through algorithmic self-policing, any malicious attempt to defraud the system would be rejected. In a precise and technical definition, Bitcoin is digital cash that is transacted via the Internet in a decentralized trustless system using a public ledger called the *blockchain*. It is a new form of money that combines BitTorrent peer-to-peer file sharing[1] with public key cryptography.[2] Since its launch in 2009, Bitcoin has spawned a group of imitators—alternative currencies using the same general approach but with different optimizations and tweaks. More important, blockchain technology could become the seamless embedded economic layer the Web has never had, serving as the technological underlay for payments, decentralized exchange, token earning and spending, digital asset invocation and transfer, and smart contract issuance and execution. Bitcoin and blockchain technology, as a mode of decentralization, could be the next major disruptive technology and worldwide computing paradigm (following the mainframe, PC, Internet, and social networking/mobile phones), with the potential for reconfiguring all human activity as pervasively as did the Web.

Currency, Contracts, and Applications beyond Financial Markets

The potential benefits of the blockchain are more than just economic—they extend into political, humanitarian, social, and scientific domains—and the technological capacity of the blockchain is already being harnessed by specific groups to address real-world problems. For example, to counter repressive political regimes, blockchain technology can be used to enact in a decentralized cloud functions that previously needed administration by jurisdictionally bound organizations. This is obviously useful for organizations like WikiLeaks (where national governments prevented credit card processors from accepting donations in the sensitive Edward Snowden situation) as well as organizations that are transnational in scope and neutral in political outlook, like Internet standards group ICANN and DNS services. Beyond these situations in which a public interest must transcend governmental power structures, other industry sectors and classes can be freed from skewed regulatory and licensing schemes subject to the hierarchical power structures and influence of strongly backed special interest groups on governments, enabling new disintermediated business models. Even though regulation spurred by the institutional lobby has effectively crippled consumer genome services,[3] newer sharing economy models like Airbnb and Uber have been standing up strongly in legal attacks from incumbents.[4]

In addition to economic and political benefits, the coordination, record keeping, and irrevocability of transactions using blockchain technology are features that could be as fundamental for forward progress in society as the Magna Carta or the Rosetta Stone. In this case, the blockchain can serve as the public records repository for whole societies, including the registry of all documents, events, identities, and assets. In this system, all property could become *smart property*; this is the notion of encoding every asset to the blockchain with a unique identifier such that the asset can be tracked, controlled, and exchanged (bought or sold) on the blockchain. This means that all manner of tangible assets (houses, cars) and digital assets could be registered and transacted on the blockchain.

As an example (we'll see more over the course of this book), we can see the world-changing potential of the blockchain in its use for registering and protecting intellectual property (IP). The emerging digital art industry offers services for privately registering the exact contents of any digital asset (any file, image, health record, software, etc.) to the blockchain. The blockchain could replace or supplement all existing IP management systems. How it works is that a standard algorithm is run over a file (any file) to compress it into a short 64-character code (called a *hash*) that is unique to that document.[5] No matter how large the file (e.g., a 9-GB genome file), it is compressed into a 64-character secure hash that cannot be computed backward. The hash is then included in a blockchain transaction, which adds the timestamp—the proof of that digital asset existing at that moment. The hash can be recalculated from the underlying file (stored privately on the owner's computer, not on the blockchain), confirming that the original contents have not changed. Standardized mechanisms such as contract law have been revolutionary steps forward for society, and blockchain IP (digital art) could be exactly one of these inflection points for the smoother coordination of large-scale societies, as more and more economic activity is driven by the creation of ideas.

Blockchain 1.0, 2.0, and 3.0

The economic, political, humanitarian, and legal system benefits of Bitcoin and blockchain technology start to make it clear that this is potentially an extremely disruptive technology that could have the capacity for reconfiguring all aspects of society and its operations. For organization and convenience, the different kinds of existing and potential activities in the blockchain revolution are broken down into three categories: Blockchain 1.0, 2.0, and 3.0. Blockchain 1.0 is *currency*, the deployment of cryptocurrencies in applications related to cash, such as currency transfer, remittance, and digital payment systems. Blockchain 2.0 is *contracts*, the entire slate of economic, market, and financial applications using the blockchain that are more extensive than simple cash transactions: stocks, bonds, futures, loans, mortgages, titles, smart property, and smart contracts. Blockchain 3.0 is blockchain *applications* beyond currency, finance, and markets—particularly in the areas of government, health, science, literacy, culture, and art.

What Is Bitcoin?

Bitcoin is digital cash. It is a digital currency and online payment system in which encryption techniques are used to regulate the generation of units of currency and verify the transfer of funds, operating independently of a central bank. The terminology can be confusing because the words *Bitcoin* and *blockchain* may be used to refer to any three parts of the concept: the underlying blockchain *technology*, the *protocol* and *client* through which transactions are effected, and the actual *cryptocurrency* (money); or also more broadly to refer to the whole concept of cryptocurrencies. It is as if PayPal had called the Internet "PayPal," upon which the PayPal protocol was run, to transfer the PayPal currency. The blockchain industry is using these terms interchangeably sometimes because it is still in the process of shaping itself into what could likely become established layers in a technology stack.

Bitcoin was created in 2009 (released on January 9, 2009[6]) by an unknown person or entity using the name Satoshi Nakamoto. The concept and operational details are described in a concise and readable white paper, "Bitcoin: A Peer-to-Peer Electronic Cash System."[7] Payments using the decentralized virtual currency are recorded in a public ledger that is stored on many—potentially all—Bitcoin users' computers, and continuously viewable on the Internet. Bitcoin is the first and largest decentralized cryptocurrency. There are hundreds of other "altcoin" (alternative coin) cryptocurrencies, like Litecoin and Dogecoin, but Bitcoin comprises 90 percent of the market capitalization of all cryptocurrencies and is the de facto standard. Bitcoin is pseudonymous (not anonymous) in the sense that public key addresses (27–32 alphanumeric character strings; similar in function to an email address) are used to send and receive Bitcoins and record transactions, as opposed to personally identifying information.

Bitcoins are created as a reward for computational processing work, known as *mining*, in which users offer their computing power to verify and record payments into the public ledger. Individuals or companies engage in mining in exchange for transaction fees and newly created Bitcoins. Besides mining, Bitcoins can, like any currency, be obtained in exchange for fiat money, products, and services. Users can send and receive Bitcoins electronically for an optional transaction fee using *wallet software* on a personal computer, mobile device, or web application.

What Is the Blockchain?

The blockchain is the public ledger of all Bitcoin transactions that have ever been executed. It is constantly growing as miners add new blocks to it (every 10 minutes) to record the most recent transactions. The blocks are added to the blockchain in a linear, chronological order. Each full node (i.e., every computer connected to the Bitcoin network using a client that performs the task of validating and relaying transactions) has a copy of the blockchain, which is downloaded automatically when the miner joins the Bitcoin network. The blockchain has complete information about addresses and balances from the genesis block (the very first transactions ever executed) to the most recently completed block. The blockchain as a public ledger means that it is easy to query any block explorer (such as *https://blockchain.info/*) for transactions associated with a particular Bitcoin address—for example, you can look up your own wallet address to see the transaction in which you received your first Bitcoin.

The blockchain is seen as the main technological innovation of Bitcoin because it stands as a "trustless" proof mechanism of all the transactions on the network. Users can trust the system of the public ledger stored worldwide on many different decentralized nodes maintained by "miner-accountants," as opposed to having to establish and maintain trust with the transaction counterparty (another person) or a third-party intermediary (like a bank). The blockchain as the architecture for a new system of *decentralized trustless transactions* is the key innovation. The blockchain allows the disintermediation and decentralization of all transactions of any type between all parties on a global basis.

The blockchain is like another application layer to run on the existing stack of Internet protocols, adding an entire new tier to the Internet to enable economic transactions, both immediate digital currency payments (in a universally usable cryptocurrency) and longer-term, more complicated financial contracts. Any currency, financial contract, or hard or soft asset may be transacted with a system like a blockchain. Further, the blockchain may be used not just for transactions, but also as a registry and inventory system for the recording, tracking, monitoring, and transacting of all assets. A blockchain is quite literally like a giant spreadsheet for registering all assets, and an accounting system for transacting them on a global scale that can include all forms of assets held by all parties worldwide. Thus, the blockchain can be used for any form of asset registry, inventory, and exchange, including every area of finance, economics, and money; hard assets (physical property); and intangible assets (votes, ideas, reputation, intention, health data, etc.).

The Connected World and Blockchain: The Fifth Disruptive Computing Paradigm

One model of understanding the modern world is through computing paradigms, with a new paradigm arising on the order of one per decade (Figure P-1). First, there were the mainframe and PC (personal computer) paradigms, and then the Internet revolutionized everything. Mobile and social networking was the most recent paradigm. The current emerging paradigm for this decade could be the *connected world of computing* relying on blockchain cryptography. The connected world could usefully include blockchain technology as the economic overlay to what is increasingly becoming a seamlessly connected world of multidevice computing that includes wearable computing, Internet-of-Things (IoT) sensors, smartphones, tablets, laptops, quantified self-tracking devices (i.e., Fitbit), smart home, smart car, and smart city. The economy that the blockchain enables is not merely the movement of money, however; it is the transfer of information and the effective allocation of resources that money has enabled in the human- and corporate-scale economy.

With revolutionary potential equal to that of the Internet, blockchain technology could be deployed and adopted much more quickly than the Internet was, given the network effects of current widespread global Internet and cellular connectivity.

Just as the social-mobile functionality of Paradigm 4 has become an expected feature of technology properties, with mobile apps for everything and sociality as a website property (liking, commenting, friending, forum participation), so too could the blockchain of Paradigm 5 bring the pervasive expectation of value exchange functionality. Paradigm 5 functionality could be the experience of a continuously connected, seamless, physical-world, multidevice computing layer, with a blockchain technology overlay for payments—not just basic payments, but micropayments, decentralized exchange, token earning and spending, digital asset invocation and transfer, and smart contract issuance and execution—as the economic layer the Web never had. The world is already being prepared for more pervasive Internet-based money: Apple Pay (Apple's token-based ewallet mobile app) and its competitors could be a critical intermediary step in moving to a full-fledged cryptocurrency world in which the blockchain becomes the seamless economic layer of the Web.

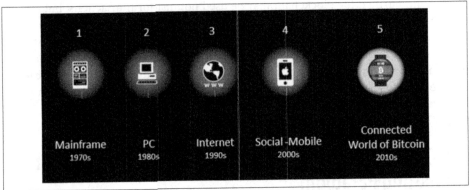

Figure P-1. Disruptive computing paradigms: Mainframe, PC, Internet, Social-Mobile, Blockchain[8]

M2M/IoT Bitcoin Payment Network to Enable the Machine Economy

Blockchain is a revolutionary paradigm for the human world, the "Internet of Individuals," and it could also be the enabling currency of the machine economy. Gartner estimates the Internet of Things will comprise 26 billion devices and a $1.9 trillion economy by 2020.[9] A corresponding "Internet of Money" cryptocurrency is needed to manage the transactions between these devices,[10] and micropayments between connected devices could develop into a new layer of the economy.[11] Cisco estimates that M2M (machine-to-machine) connections are growing faster than any other category (84 percent), and that not only is global IP traffic forecast to grow threefold from 2012 to 2018, but the composition is shifting in favor of mobile, WiFi, and M2M traffic.[12] Just as a money economy allows for better, faster, and more efficient allocation of resources on a human scale, a machine economy can provide a robust and decentralized system of handling these same issues on a machine scale.

Some examples of interdevice micropayments could be connected automobiles automatically negotiating higher-speed highway passage if they are in a hurry, microcompensating road peers on a more relaxed schedule. Coordinating personal air delivery drones is another potential use case for device-to-device micropayment networks where individual priorities can be balanced. Agricultural sensors are an example of another type of system that can use economic principles to filter out routine irrelevant data but escalate priority data when environmental threshold conditions (e.g., for humidity) have been met by a large enough group of sensors in a deployed swarm.

Blockchain technology's decentralized model of trustless peer-to-peer transactions means, at its most basic level, intermediary-free transactions. However, the potential shift to decentralized trustless transactions on a large-scale global basis for every sort of interaction and transaction (human-to-human, human-to-machine, machine-to-machine) could imply a dramatically different structure and operation of society in ways that cannot yet be foreseen but where current established power relationships and hierarchies could easily lose their utility.

Mainstream Adoption: Trust, Usability, Ease of Use

Because many of the ideas and concepts behind Bitcoin and blockchain technology are new and technically intricate, one complaint has been that perhaps cryptocurrencies are too complicated for mainstream adoption. However, the same was true of the Internet, and more generally at the beginning of any new technology era, the technical details of "what it is" and "how it works" are of interest to a popular audience. This is not a real barrier; it is not necessary to know how TCP/IP works in order to send an email, and new technology applications pass into public use without much further consideration of the technical details as long as appropriate, usable, trustable frontend applications are developed. For example, not all users need to see (much less manually type) the gory detail of a 32-character alphanumeric public address. Already "mainstream wallet" companies such as Circle Internet Financial and Xapo are developing frontend applications specifically targeted at the mainstream adoption of Bitcoin (with the goal of being the "Gmail of Bitcoin" in terms of frontend usability—and market share). Because Bitcoin and ewallets are related to money, there is obvious additional sensitivity in end-user applications and consumer trust that services need to establish. There are many cryptocurrency security issues to address to engender a crypto-literate public with usable customer wallets, including how to back up your money, what to do if you lose your private key, and what to do if you received a proscribed (i.e., previously stolen) coin in a transaction and now cannot get rid of it. However, these issues are being addressed by the blockchain industry, and alternative currencies can take advantage of being just another node in the ongoing progression of financial technology (fintech) that includes ATMs, online banking, and now Apple Pay.

Currency application adoption could be straightforward with trustable usable frontends, but the successful mainstream adoption of beyond-currency blockchain applications could be subtler. For example, virtual notary services seem like a no-brainer for the easy, low-cost, secure, permanent, findable registration of IP, contracts, wills, and similar documents. There will doubtlessly remain social reasons that people prefer to interact with a lawyer about certain matters (perhaps the human-based advice, psychoanalysis, or validation function that attorneys may provide), and for these kinds of reasons, technology adoption based exclusively on efficiency arguments could falter. Overall, however, if Bitcoin and the blockchain industry are to mature, it will most likely be in phases, similar to the adoption pattern of the Internet for which a clear value proposition resonated with different potential audiences, and then they came online with the new technology. Initially, the Internet solved collaborative research problems for a subgroup: academic researchers and the military. Then, gamers and avid recreational users came online, and eventually, everyone. In the case of Bitcoin, so far the early adopters are subcultures of people concerned about money and ideology, and the next steps for widespread adoption could be as blockchain technology solves practical problems for other large groups of people, For example, some leading subgroups for whom blockchain technology solves a major issue include those affected by Internet censorship in repressive political regimes, where decentralized blockchain DNS (domain name system) services could make a big difference. Likewise, in the IP market, blockchain technology could be employed to register the chain of invention for patents, and revolutionize IP litigation in the areas of asset custody, access, and attribution.

Bitcoin Culture: Bitfilm Festival

One measure of any new technology's crossover into mainstream adoption is how it is taken up in popular culture. An early indication that the cryptocurrency industry may be starting to arrive in the global social psyche is the Bitfilm Festival (*http://bitfilm.com/festival.html*), which features films with Bitcoin-related content. Films are selected that demonstrate the universal yet culturally distinct interpretations and impact of Bitcoin. The festival began in 2013 and has late 2014/early 2015 dates in Berlin (where Bitfilm (*http://bitfilm.com/*) is based), Seoul, Buenos Aires, Amsterdam, Rio, and Cape Town. Congruently, Bitfilm allows viewers to vote for their favorite films with Bitcoin. Bitfilm produces the film festival and, in another business line, makes promotional videos for the blockchain industry (Figure P-2).

Figure P-2. Bitfilm promotional videos

Intention, Methodology, and Structure of this Book

The blockchain industry is nascent and currently (late 2014) in a phase of tremendous dynamism and innovation. Concepts, terminology, standards, key players, norms, and industry attitudes toward certain projects are changing rapidly. It could be that even a year from now, we look back and see that Bitcoin and blockchain technology in its current instantiation has become defunct, superseded, or otherwise rendered an artifact of the past. As an example, one area with significant evolving change is the notion of the appropriate security for consumer ewallets—not an insubstantial concern given the hacking raids that can plague the cryptocurrency industry. The current ewallet security standard is now widely thought to be *multisig* (using multiple key signatures to approve a transaction), but most users (still early adopters, not mainstream) have not yet upgraded to this level of security.

This book is intended as an exploration of the broader concepts, features, and functionality of Bitcoin and blockchain technology, and their future possibilities and implications; it does not support, advocate, or offer any advice or prediction as to the industry's viability. Further, this text is intended as a presentation and discussion of advanced concepts, because there are many other "Blockchain 101" resources available. The blockchain industry is in an emergent and immature phase and very much still in development with many risks. Given this dynamism, despite our best efforts, there may be errors in the specific details of this text whereas even a few days from now information might be outdated; the intent here is to portray the *general* scope and status of the blockchain industry and its possibilities. Right now is the time to learn about the underlying technologies; their potential uses, dangers, and risks; and perhaps more importantly, the concepts and their extensibility. The objective here is to provide a comprehensive overview of the nature, scope, and type of activity that is occurring in the cryptocurrency industry and envision its wide-ranging potential application. The account is necessarily incomplete, prone to technical errors (though it has been reviewed for technical accuracy by experts), and, again, could likely soon be out-of-date as different projects described here fail or succeed. Or, the entire Bitcoin and blockchain technology industry as currently conceived could become outmoded or superseded by other models.

The underlying sources of this work are a variety of information resources related to Bitcoin and its development. The principal sources are developer forums, Reddit subgroups, GitHub white papers, podcasts, news media, YouTube, blogs, and Twitter. Specific online resources include Bitcoin industry conference proceedings on YouTube and Slideshare, podcasts (Let's Talk Bitcoin, Consider This!, Epicenter Bitcoin), EtherCasts (Ethereum), Bitcoin-related news outlets (*CoinDesk, Bitcoin Magazine, Cryptocoins News, Coin Telegraph*), and forums (Bitcoin StackExchange, Quora). Other sources were email exchanges and conversations with practitioners in the industry as well as my experiences attending conferences, Bitcoin workshops, Satoshi Square trading sessions, and developer meetups.

This work is structured to discuss three different tiers in the way that the conceptualization of Bitcoin and blockchain technology is starting to gel: Blockchain 1.0, 2.0, and 3.0. First, I cover the basic definitions and concepts of Bitcoin and blockchain technology, and currency and payments as the core Blockchain 1.0 applications. Second, I describe Blockchain 2.0—market and financial applications beyond currency, such as contracts. I then envision Blockchain 3.0, meaning blockchain applications beyond currency, finance, and markets. Within this broad category are justice applications such as blockchain governance, uplifting organizations (like WikiLeaks, ICANN, and

DNS services) away from repressive jurisdictional regimes to the decentralized cloud, protection of IP, and digital identity verification and authentication. Fourth, I consider another class of Blockchain 3.0 applications beyond currency, finance, and markets, for which the blockchain model offers scale, efficiency, organization, and coordination benefits in the areas of science, genomics, health, learning, academic publishing, development, aid, and culture. Finally, I present advanced concepts like demurrage (incitory) currency, and consider them in the greater context of the wide-scale deployment of blockchain technology.

Safari® Books Online

 *Safari Books Online* is an on-demand digital library that delivers expert content in both book and video form from the world's leading authors in technology and business.

Technology professionals, software developers, web designers, and business and creative professionals use Safari Books Online as their primary resource for research, problem solving, learning, and certification training.

Safari Books Online offers a range of plans and pricing for enterprise, government, education, and individuals.

Members have access to thousands of books, training videos, and prepublication manuscripts in one fully searchable database from publishers like O'Reilly Media, Prentice Hall Professional, Addison-Wesley Professional, Microsoft Press, Sams, Que, Peachpit Press, Focal Press, Cisco Press, John Wiley & Sons, Syngress, Morgan Kaufmann, IBM Redbooks, Packt, Adobe Press, FT Press, Apress, Manning, New Riders, McGraw-Hill, Jones & Bartlett, Course Technology, and hundreds more. For more information about Safari Books Online, please visit us online.

How to Contact Us

Please address comments and questions concerning this book to the publisher:

O'Reilly Media, Inc.
1005 Gravenstein Highway North
Sebastopol, CA 95472
800-998-9938 (in the United States or Canada)
707-829-0515 (international or local)
707-829-0104 (fax)

We have a web page for this book, where we list errata, examples, and any additional information. You can access this page at *http://bit.ly/blockchain_1e*.

To comment or ask technical questions about this book, send email to *bookquestions@oreilly.com*.

For more information about our books, courses, conferences, and news, see our website at *http://www.oreilly.com*.

Find us on Facebook: *http://facebook.com/oreilly*

Follow us on Twitter: *http://twitter.com/oreillymedia*

Watch us on YouTube: *http://www.youtube.com/oreillymedia*

Acknowledgments

I would like to acknowledge Andreas M. Antonopoulos, Trent McConaghy, Steve Omohundro, Piotr Piasecki, Justin Sher, Chris Tse, and Stephan Tual.

CHAPTER 1

Blockchain 1.0: Currency

Technology Stack: Blockchain, Protocol, Currency

Bitcoin terminology can be confusing because the word *Bitcoin* is used to simultaneously denote three different things. First, Bitcoin refers to the underlying blockchain technology platform. Second, Bitcoin is used to mean the protocol that runs over the underlying blockchain technology to describe how assets are transferred on the blockchain. Third, Bitcoin denotes a digital currency, Bitcoin, the first and largest of the cryptocurrencies.

Table 1-1 demonstrates a helpful way to distinguish the different uses. The first layer is the underlying technology, the blockchain. The blockchain is the decentralized transparent ledger with the transaction records—the database that is shared by all network nodes, updated by miners, monitored by everyone, and owned and controlled by no one. It is like a giant interactive spreadsheet that everyone has access to and updates and confirms that the digital transactions transferring funds are unique.

The middle tier of the stack is the protocol—the software system that transfers the money over the blockchain ledger. Then, the top layer is the currency itself, Bitcoin, which is denoted as *BTC* or *Btc* when traded in transactions or exchanges. There are hundreds of cryptocurrencies, of which Bitcoin is the first and largest. Others include Litecoin, Dogecoin, Ripple, NXT, and Peercoin; the major alt-currencies can be tracked at *http://coinmarketcap.com/*.

Table 1-1. Layers in the technology stack of the Bitcoin blockchain

Cryptocurrency: Bitcoin (BTC), Litecoin, Dogecoin

Bitcoin protocol and client: Software programs that conduct transactions

Bitcoin blockchain: Underlying decentralized ledger

The key point is that these three layers are the general structure of any modern cryptocurrency: blockchain, protocol, and currency. Each coin is typically both a currency and a protocol, and it may have its own blockchain or may run on the Bitcoin blockchain. For example, the Litecoin currency runs on the Litecoin protocol, which runs on the Litecoin blockchain. (Litecoin is very slightly adapted from Bitcoin to improve on a few features.) A separate blockchain means that the coin has its own decentralized ledger (in the same structure and format as the Bitcoin blockchain ledger). Other protocols, such as Counterparty, have their own currency (XCP) and run on the Bitcoin blockchain (i.e., their transactions are registered in the Bitcoin blockchain ledger). A spreadsheet delineating some of the kinds of differences between Crypto 2.0 projects is maintained here: *http://bit.ly/crypto_2_0_comp*.

The Double-Spend and Byzantine Generals' Computing Problems

Even without considering the many possible uses of Bitcoin and blockchain technology, Bitcoin, at its most fundamental level, is a core breakthrough in computer science, one that builds on 20 years of research into cryptographic currency, and 40 years of research in cryptography, by thousands of researchers around the world.[13] Bitcoin is a solution to a long-standing issue with digital cash: the *double-spend problem*. Until blockchain cryptography, digital cash was, like any other digital asset, infinitely copiable (like our ability to save an email attachment any number of times), and there was no way to confirm that a certain batch of digital cash had not already been spent without a central intermediary. There had to be a trusted third party (whether a bank or a quasibank like PayPal) in transactions, which kept a ledger confirming that each portion of digital cash was spent only once; this is the double-spend problem. A related computing challenge is the Byzantine Generals' Problem, connoting the difficulty of multiple parties (generals) on the battlefield not trusting each other but needing to have some sort of coordinated communication mechanism.[14]

The blockchain solves the double-spend problem by combining BitTorrent peer-to-peer file-sharing technology with public-key cryptography to make a new form of digital money. Coin ownership is recorded in the public ledger and confirmed by cryptographic protocols and the mining community. The blockchain is trustless in the sense that a user does not need to trust the other party in the transaction, or a central intermediary, but does need to trust the system: the blockchain protocol software system. The "blocks" in the chain are groups of transactions posted sequentially to the ledger—that is, added to the "chain." Blockchain ledgers can be inspected publicly with *block explorers*, Internet sites (e.g., *www.Blockchain.info* for the Bitcoin blockchain) where you can see a transaction stream by entering a blockchain address (a user's public-key address, like *1DpZHXi5bEjNn6SriUKjh6wE4HwPFBPvfx*).

How a Cryptocurrency Works

Bitcoin is money, digital cash, a way of buying and selling things over the Internet. The Bitcoin value chain is composed of several different constituencies: software developers, miners, exchanges, merchant processing services, web wallet companies, and users/consumers. From an individual user's perspective, the important elements in transacting coin (I'll use "coin" in the generic sense here) are an address, a private key, and wallet software. The address is where others can send Bitcoin to you, and the private key is the cryptographic secret by which you can send Bitcoin to others. Wallet software is the software you run on your own computer to manage your Bitcoin (see Figure 1-1). There is no centralized "account" you need to register with another company; if you have the private key to an address, you can use that private key to access the coin associated with that address from any Internet-connected computer (including, of course, smartphones). Wallet software can also keep a copy of the blockchain—the record of all the transactions that have occurred in that currency—as part of the decentralized scheme by which coin transactions are verified. Appendix A covers the practicalities of maintaining an altcoin wallet in more detail.

Figure 1-1. Bitcoin ewallet app and transferring Bitcoin (image credits: Bitcoin ewallet developers and InterAksyon)

eWallet Services and Personal Cryptosecurity

As responsible consumers, we are not used to many of the new aspects of blockchain technology and personal cryptosecurity; for example, having to back up our money. Decentralized autonomy in the form of private keys stored securely in your ewallet means that there is no customer service number to call for password recovery or private key backup. If your private key is gone, your Bitcoin is gone. This could be an indication that blockchain technology is not yet mature enough for mainstream adoption; it's the kind of problem that consumer-facing Bitcoin startups such as Circle Internet Financial and Xapo are trying to solve. There is opportunity for some sort of standardized app or service for ewallet backup (for example, for lost, stolen, bricked, or upgraded smartphones or laptop/tablet-based wallets), with which users can confirm exactly what is happening with their private keys in the backup service, whether they self-administer it or rely on external vendors. Personal cryptosecurity is a significant new area for consumer literacy, because the stakes are quite high to ensure that personal financial assets and transactions are protected in this new online venue of digital cash. Another element of personal cryptosecurity that many experts recommend is *coin mixing*, pooling your coins with other transactions so that they are more anonymous, using services like Dark Coin, Dark Wallet, and BitMixer.[15] As the marketplace of alternative currencies grows, demand for a unified ewallet will likely rise, because installing a new and separate wallet is required for most blockchain-related services, and it is easy to have 20 different ewallets crowding your smartphone.

Despite their current clunkiness in implementation, cryptocurrencies offer many great benefits in personal cryptosecurity. One of the great advantages is that block-chain is a *push technology* (the user initiates and pushes relevant information to the network for this transaction only), not a *pull technology* (like a credit card or bank for which the user's personal information is on file to be pulled any time it is authorized). Credit card technology was not developed to be secure on the Internet the way that blockchain models are developing now. Pull technology requires having datastores of customer personal information that are essentially centralized honey pots, increasingly vulnerable to hacker identity theft attacks (Target, Chase, and Dairy Queen are just a few recent examples of large-scale identity-theft vendor database raids). Paying with Bitcoin at any of the 30,000 vendors that accept it as of October 2014 (e.g., Overstock, New Egg, and Dell Computer; see *https://bitpay.com/directory#/*) means not having to entrust your personal financial information to centralized vendor databases. It might also possibly entail a lower transaction fee (Bitcoin transaction fees are much lower than merchant credit card processing fees).

Merchant Acceptance of Bitcoin

At the time of writing, the main Bitcoin merchant processing solutions for vendors to accept Bitcoin are BitPay (*http://www.bitpay.com*) and Coinbase (*https://www.coinbase.com/*) in the United States, and Coinify (*http://www.coinify.com*) in Europe.[16] However, it is difficult for vendors, like the local café, to run two separate payment systems (traditional and Bitcoin), so a more expedient future solution would involve integrating Bitcoin payment into existing vendor payment networks. Mobile payment functionality is also needed for quick point-of-sale Bitcoin purchases (for example, a cup of coffee) via mobile phone. CoinBeyond (*http://www.coinbeyond.com/*) and other companies focus on mobile Bitcoin payments specifically, and BitPay and Coin-Base have solutions for mobile checkout (*https://bitpay.com/bitcoin-for-retail*). In one notable step forward, Intuit's QuickBooks accounting software for small businesses makes it possible for vendors to accept incoming Bitcoin payments from CoinBase and BitPay with its PayByCoin module (*http://bit.ly/paybycoin*).[17]

Summary: Blockchain 1.0 in Practical Use

Blockchain is already cash for the Internet, a digital payment system, and it may become the "Internet of Money," connecting finances in the way that the Internet of Things (IoT) connects machines. Currency and payments make up the first and most obvious application. Alternative currencies make sense based on an economic argument alone: reducing worldwide credit card merchant payment fees from as much as 3 percent to below 1 percent has obvious benefits for the economy, especially in the $514 billion international remittances market, where transaction fees can run from 7 to 30 percent.[18] Furthermore, users can receive funds immediately in digital wallets instead of waiting days for transfers. Bitcoin and its imitators could pave the way for currency, trade, and commerce as we know it to be completely redefined. More broadly, Bitcoin is not just a better version of Visa—it could also allow us to do things we have not even thought of yet. Currency and payments is just the first application.[19] The core functionality of blockchain currencies is that any transaction can be sourced and completed directly between two individuals over the Internet. With altcoins, you can allocate and trade resources between individuals in a completely decentralized, distributed, and global way. With that ability, a cryptocurrency can be a programmable open network for the decentralized trading of all resources, well beyond currency and payments. Thus, Blockchain 1.0 for currency and payments is already being extended into Blockchain 2.0 to take advantage of the more robust functionality of Bitcoin as programmable money.

Relation to Fiat Currency

Considering Bitcoin as the paradigm and most widely adopted case, the price of Bitcoin is $399.40 as of November 12, 2014. The price has ranged considerably (as you can see in Figure 1-2), from $12 at the beginning of 2013 to a high of $1,242 per coin on November 29, 2013 (trading higher than gold—$1,240 per ounce—that day).[20] That peak was the culmination of a few factors: the Cyprus banking crisis (March 2013) drove a great deal of demand, for example. The price was also driven up by heavy trading in China until December 5, 2013, when the Chinese government banned institutions (but not individuals) from handling Bitcoin, after which the price fell.[21] In 2014, the price has declined gradually from $800 to its present value of approximately $350 in December 2014. An oft-reported though disputed metric is that 70 percent of Bitcoin trades are made up of Chinese Yuan.[22] It is difficult to evaluate how much of that figure indicates meaningful economic activity because the Chinese exchanges do not charge trade fees, and therefore people can trade any amount of currency back and forth for free, creating fake volume. Further, much of the Yuan-denominated trade must be speculation (as is true for overall Bitcoin trade), as there are few physical-world vendors accepting Bitcoin and few consumers using the currency for the widespread consumption of goods and services.

Figure 1-2. Bitcoin price 2009 through November 2014 (source: http://coinmarket cap.com/currencies/bitcoin/#charts)

Some argue that volatility and price shifts are a barrier to the widespread adoption of cryptocurrency, and some volatility-smoothing businesses have launched to address this: Bitreserve (*https://bitreserve.org*), which locks Bitcoin deposits at fixed exchange rates;[23] Realcoin (*http://realcoin.com*)'s cryptocurrency, which is pegged to the US dollar (USD);[24] and Coinapult's LOCKS (*https://coinapult.com/locks/info*), which allow purchasers to peg Bitcoin to the price of gold, silver, the US dollar, the British pound, or the Euro.[25] One of the first USD-pegged Bitcoin cryptocurrencies was Ripple's XRP/USD BitStamp (*https://www.ripplecharts.com/*), and there is also BitShares' BitUSD (*http://wiki.bitshares.org/index.php/BitShares/Market_Peg*). Others point out that Bitcoin volatility is less than some fiat currency's volatility and inflation (making Bitcoin a better relative value choice), and that many operations of Bitcoin are immediate transfers in and out of other currencies for which the volatility does not matter as much in these spot rate (i.e., immediate) transactions.

Bitcoin's market capitalization as of November 2014 is $5.3 billion (see *http://coinmar ketcap.com/*), calculated as the current price ($399.40) multiplied by the available supply (13,492,000 Bitcoin). This is already on the order of a small country's GDP (Bitcoin would rank as the 150th largest world economy on a list of 200). Unlike fiat currencies for which governments can print more money, the money supply of Bitcoin grows at a predetermined (and capped) rate. New currency (in blocks) is being issued at a regular and known pace, with about 13.5 million units currently outstanding, growing to a capped amount of 21 million units in 2040. At a price of roughly $400 Bitcoin per dollar, Bitcoin is infeasible to use directly for daily purchases, and prices and exchanges for practical use are typically denominated in subunits of *millibitcoins* (a thousandth of a Bitcoin; 1 mBTC = ~$0.40) and *Satoshis* (a millionth of a Bitcoin; 1 Satoshi = ~$0.000004).

Regulatory Status

Government regulation is possibly one of the most significant factors as to whether the blockchain industry will develop into a full-fledged financial-services industry. As of October 2013, a handful of countries (*http://bit.ly/bitcoin_by_country*) have completely banned Bitcoin: Bangladesh, Bolivia, Ecuador, Iceland (possibly related to using Auroracoin, instead), Kyrgyzstan, and Vietnam. China, as mentioned, banned financial institutions from dealing in the virtual currency as of December 2013, although trading volume in Chinese Yuan persists.[26] Germany, France, Korea, and Thailand have all looked unfavorably on Bitcoin.[27] The European Banking Authority, Switzerland, Poland, Canada, and the United States continue to deliberate about different Bitcoin-related issues.[28] Countries try to match up Bitcoin (and the concept of digital currencies) to their existing regulatory structures, often finding that cryptocurrencies do not quite fit and ultimately concluding that cryptocurrencies are sufficiently different that new legislation might be required. At present, some countries, like the UK, have classified Bitcoin as a currency (and therefore not subject to VAT), whereas other countries, like Australia, were not able to classify Bitcoin as a currency due to laws about nationalized issuance (and Bitcoin therefore is subject to VAT or GST—the goods and services tax).[29]

In the United States, the Internal Revenue Service treats Bitcoin as property (like stock) and not as money, meaning that users of Bitcoin are liable for capital gains taxes on transactions.[30] For taxation, virtual currencies are property, not currency. However, nearly every other US government agency—including FinCEN (financial crimes enforcement network), banking regulators, and the CFPB, SEC, CFTC, and DOJ—regulate Bitcoin as a currency.[31]

CHAPTER 2

Blockchain 2.0: Contracts

From its very beginning, complexity beyond currency and payments was envisioned for Bitcoin; the possibilities for programmable money and contracts were baked into the protocol at its invention. A 2010 communication from Satoshi Nakamoto indicates that "the design supports a tremendous variety of possible transaction types that I designed years ago. Escrow transactions, bonded contracts, third-party arbitration, multiparty signature, etc. If Bitcoin catches on in a big way, these are things we'll want to explore in the future, but they all had to be designed at the beginning to make sure they would be possible later."[32] As we'll see in Chapter 3, these structures could be applied beyond financial transactions, to any kind of transaction—even "figurative" ones. This is because the concepts and structure developed for Bitcoin are extremely portable and extensible.

Blockchain 2.0 is the next big tier in the development of the blockchain industry, an area of prodigious activity as of the fall of 2014.[33] Because the Blockchain 2.0 space is in development, there are many different categories, distinctions, and understandings of it, and standard classifications and definitions are still emerging. Some of the terminology that broadly refers to the Blockchain 2.0 space can include Bitcoin 2.0, Bitcoin 2.0 protocols, smart contracts, smart property, Dapps (decentralized applications), DAOs (decentralized autonomous organizations), and DACs (decentralized autonomous corporations).

Whereas Blockchain 1.0 is for the decentralization of money and payments, Blockchain 2.0 is for the decentralization of markets more generally, and contemplates the transfer of many other kinds of assets beyond currency using the blockchain, from the creation of a unit of value through every time it is transferred or divided.

An approximate technological metaphor for Bitcoin is that it is analogous to the protocol stack of the Web. After the underlying Internet technology and infrastructure was in place, services could be built to run on top of it—Amazon, Netflix, and

Airbnb—becoming increasingly sophisticated over time and always adding new ways to take advantage of the underlying technology. Blockchain 1.0 has been likened to the underlying TCP/IP transport layer of the Web, with the opportunity now available to build 2.0 protocols on top of it (as HTTP, SMTP, and FTP were in the Internet model). Blockchain 2.0 protocols either literally use the Bitcoin blockchain or create their own separate blockchains, but are in the same cryptocurrency decentralized technical architecture model of the three-layer stack: blockchain, protocol, and currency. However, it is important to note that these "new Internet plumbing layers" are very much still in development and any metaphor might become quickly outdated. These analogies might be like calling Chrome a "Napster 2.0," or Facebook or AdBlock a "Web Browser 3.0."

The key idea is that the decentralized transaction ledger functionality of the blockchain could be used to register, confirm, and transfer all manner of contracts and property. Table 2-1 lists some of the different classes and examples of property and contracts that might be transferred with the blockchain. Satoshi Nakamoto started by specifying escrow transactions, bonded contracts, third-party arbitration, and multiparty signature transactions. All financial transactions could be reinvented on the blockchain, including stock, private equity, crowdfunding instruments, bonds, mutual funds, annuities, pensions, and all manner of derivatives (futures, options, swaps, and other derivatives).

Table 2-1. Blockchain applications beyond currency (adapted from the Ledra Capital Mega Master Blockchain List; see Appendix B)[34]

Class	Examples
General	Escrow transactions, bonded contracts, third-party arbitration, multiparty signature transactions
Financial transactions	Stock, private equity, crowdfunding, bonds, mutual funds, derivatives, annuities, pensions
Public records	Land and property titles, vehicle registrations, business licenses, marriage certificates, death certificates
Identification	Driver's licenses, identity cards, passports, voter registrations
Private records	IOUs, loans, contracts, bets, signatures, wills, trusts, escrows
Attestation	Proof of insurance, proof of ownership, notarized documents
Physical asset keys	Home, hotel rooms, rental cars, automobile access
Intangible assets	Patents, trademarks, copyrights, reservations, domain names

Public records, too, can be migrated to the blockchain: land and property titles, vehicle registrations, business licenses, marriage certificates, and death certificates. Digital identity can be confirmed with the blockchain through securely encoded driver's licenses, identity cards, passports, and voter registrations. Private records such as IOUs, loans, contracts, bets, signatures, wills, trusts, and escrows can be stored. Attestation can be executed via the blockchain for proof of insurance, proof of ownership, and notarized documents. Physical asset keys (which is explored further in Chapter 3) can be encoded as digital assets on the blockchain for controlled access to homes, hotel rooms, rental cars, and privately owned or shared-access automobiles (e.g., Getaround). Intangible assets (e.g., patents, trademarks, copyrights, reservations, and domain names) can also be protected and transferred via the blockchain. For example, to protect an idea, instead of trademarking it or patenting it, you could encode it to the blockchain and you would have proof of a specific cargo being registered with a specific datetime stamp for future proof (as is discussed in "Digital Art: Blockchain Attestation Services (Notary, Intellectual Property Protection)" on page 39).

Financial Services

A prime area for blockchain businesses is interfacing cryptocurrencies with traditional banking and financial markets. Venture capital–backed Ripple Labs is using blockchain technology to reinvent the banking ecosystem and allow traditional financial institutions to conduct their own business more efficiently. Ripple's payment network lets banks transfer funds and foreign exchange transactions directly between themselves without a third-party intermediary, as is now required: "Regional banks can now move money bilaterally to other regional banks without having to relay those funds through an intermediary."[35] Ripple is also developing a smart contracts platform and language, Codius (*http://codius.org/*). Another potential symbiosis between the traditional banking industry and Bitcoin is exemplified by Spanish bank Bankinter's Innovation Foundation investment in Coinffeine (*http://www.coin ffeine.com/*), a Bitcoin technology startup that aims to make it possible for end users to buy and sell Bitcoin directly without an exchange.[36]

Other businesses are also connecting Bitcoin to traditional financial and payments market solutions. PayPal is an instructive example because its development as a platform has parallels with Bitcoin, and it is on the Bitcoin adoption curve itself. PayPal was initially an innovative payments market solution outside of the traditional financial-services market, like Bitcoin, but has since become a more formal business within the regulated industry, collecting and validating detailed personal information about its customers. PayPal had been known for being on the edge of financial innovation, but it then became more corporate focused and lost the possibility of providing early market leadership with regard to Bitcoin. Now, PayPal has been incorporating Bitcoin slowly, as of September 2014 announcing partnerships with three major Bitcoin payment processors: BitPay, Coinbase, and GoCoin.[37] Also in September 2014, Paypal's Braintree unit (acquired in 2013), a mobile payments provider, is apparently working on a feature with which customers can pay for Airbnb rentals and Uber car rides with Bitcoin.[38]

In the same area of regulation-compliant Bitcoin complements to traditional financial services is the notion of a "Bitbank." Bitcoin exchange Kraken (*https://www.kraken.com/*) has partnered with a bank to provide regulated financial services involving Bitcoin.[39] There is a clear need for an analog to and innovation around traditional financial products and services for Bitcoin—for example, Bitcoin savings accounts and lending (perhaps through user-selected rules regarding fractional reserve levels). BTCjam (*https://btcjam.com/*) is an example of such decentralized blockchain-based peer-to-peer lending. Tera Exchange (*http://teraexchange.com/*) launched the first US-regulated Bitcoin swaps exchange, which could make it possible for institutional and individual investors to buy Bitcoin contracts directly through its online trading platforms. Part of the offering includes an institutional Bitcoin price index, the Tera Bitcoin Price Index, to be used as the benchmark for trading USD/XBT contracts.[40] In the same space, startup Vaurum (*https://vaurum.com/*) is building an API for financial institutions to offer traditional brokerage investors and bank customers access to Bitcoin. Another project is startup Buttercoin (*https://butter coin.com*), a Bitcoin trading platform and exchange for high-volume transactions (200,000–500,000 Bitcoin, or $70–$175 million), targeted at a business clientele who has a need to complete large-scale Bitcoin transactions.[41] Buttercoin is partnered with capital markets firm Wedbush Securities, itself one of the first security analysts to cover Bitcoin and accept Bitcoin payments for its research.

Other ventures are more radically positioned against artificial unregulated monopolies in the current stock trading market infrastructure, like the Depository Trust Company and the National Securities Clearing Corporation, or DTCC (*http://www.dtcc.com/*), which is involved in the clearing and settlement of securities. Overstock CEO Patrick Byrne and Counterparty created a new venture, Medici, announced in October 2014, to provide a decentralized stock market for equity securities in the blockchain model.[42]

Crowdfunding

Another prime example of how financial services are being reinvented with blockchain-based decentralized models is crowdfunding. The idea is that peer-to-peer fundraising models such as Kickstarter can supplant the need for traditional venture capital funding for startups. Where previously a centralized service like Kickstarter or Indiegogo was needed to enable a crowdfunding campaign, crowdfunding platforms powered by blockchain technology remove the need for an intermediary third party. Blockchain-based crowdfunding platforms make it possible for startups to raise funds by creating their own digital currencies and selling "cryptographic shares" to early backers. Investors in a crowdfunding campaign receive tokens that represent shares of the startup they support.[43]

Some of the leading cryptocurrency crowdfunding platforms include Swarm (*https:// www.swarm.co/*), an incubator of digital currency–focused startups that raised $1 million in its own crowdfunding, completed in July 2014.[44] Holding the company's own cryptocurrency, Swarmcoin, gives investors rights to the dividends from the startups in the incubator's portfolio.[45] Swarm has five projects comprising its first class of funded applications: Manna, a developer of smart personal drone networks; Coinspace, an operator of a decentralized cryptocurrency workplace; Swarmops, a decentralized organizational management software platform; Judobaby, a decentralized gaming platform; and DDP, a decentralized dance-party entertainment concept.[46] Another crowdfunding platform is Koinify (*https://koinify.com/*), whose one project so far is the Gems (*http://getgems.org/*) decentralized social network. Koinify is linked with the Melotic wallet/asset exchange platform (*https://www.melotic.com/*) to curate a decentralized application marketplace.[47] Ironically, or perhaps as a sign of the symbiotic times, Koinify raised $1 million in traditional venture capital finance to start its crowdfunding platform.[48] Another project is Lighthouse (*http://bit.ly/lh_project*), which aims to enable its users to run crowdfunding or assurance contracts directly from within a Bitcoin wallet. In Japan, a Bitcoin crowdfunding site, bitFlyer, has launched as part of the general crowdfunding site fundFlyer (*http:// fundflyer.bitflyer.jp/*).[49]

Crowdfunding is a high-profile topic at Bitcoin industry conferences, and experts argue over its legality. Opponents complain that there is currently no legal way to do crowdfunding whereby one actually owns shares in the underlying organization, and there may be different ways in which crowdfunding violates securities laws. The workaround offered by crowdfunding platforms like Swarm and Koinify, as well as one-off crowdfundings like Ethereum is to sell nonshare items, such as early access to software. However, this is somewhat disingenuous because in many cases the marketing still looks a lot like selling shares. The result is that there can be de facto investors in cryptocurrency projects who are not getting much more than early access to open source software. A better way to crowdfund cryptocurrency projects in a decentralized yet legal way, with more effective checks and balances, is needed.

Bitcoin Prediction Markets

One example of new tech with old tech is Bitcoin prediction markets like Predictious (*https://www.predictious.com/*) and Fairlay (*https://www.fairlay.com/*).[50] Bitcoin prediction markets offer a betting venue for the usual real-world outcomes as prediction markets always have, such as elections, political legislation, sports matches, and technology product releases, and also serve as a good source of information about the developing blockchain industry. Bitcoin prediction markets are one way to see what insiders think about Bitcoin's future price directions, the success of different altcoin and protocol 2.0 projects, and industry issues more generally (e.g., technical development issues with Bitcoin, such as when there will be a hard fork—significant change—of the code, and the level of difficulty of the mining algorithm).

Smart Property

The blockchain can be used for any form of asset registry, inventory, and exchange, including every area of finance, economics, and money; hard assets (physical property); and intangible assets (votes, ideas, reputation, intention, health data, and information). Using blockchain technology this way opens up multiple classes of application functionality across all segments of businesses involved in money, markets, and financial transactions. Blockchain-encoded property becomes smart property that is transactable via smart contracts.

The general concept of smart property is the notion of transacting all property in blockchain-based models. Property could be physical-world hard assets like a home, car, bicycle, or computer, or intangible assets such as stock shares, reservations, or copyrights (e.g., books, music, illustrations, and digital fine art). An example of using the blockchain to control and transfer limited-run artworks is Swancoin (*http://bit.ly/ swancoin*), where 121 physical-world artworks, crafted on 30 × 30 cm varnished plywood, are available for purchase and transfer via the Bitcoin blockchain (see Figure 2-1).[51] Any asset can be registered in the blockchain, and thus its ownership can be controlled by whoever has the private key. The owner can then sell the asset by transferring the private key to another party. *Smart property*, then, is property whose ownership is controlled via the blockchain, using contracts subject to existing law. For example, a pre-established smart contract could automatically transfer the ownership of a vehicle title from the financing company to the individual owner when all the loan payments have been made (as automatically confirmed by other blockchain-based smart contracts). Similarly, mortgage interest rates could reset automatically per another blockchain-based smart contract checking a prespecified and contract-encoded website or data element for obtaining the interest rate on certain future days.

Figure 2-1. Swancoin: limited-circulation digital asset artwork (image credit: http://swan coin.tumblr.com/)

The key idea of smart property is controlling ownership and access to an asset by having it registered as a digital asset on the blockchain and having access to the private key. In some cases, physical-world hard assets could quite literally be controlled with the blockchain. Smartphones could unlock upon reaffirming a user's digital identity encoded in the blockchain. The doors of physical property such as vehicles and homes could be "smartmatter"-enabled through embedded technology (e.g., software code, sensors, QR codes, NFC tags, iBeacons, WiFi access, etc.) so that access could be controlled in real time as users seeking entry present their own hardware or software token to match that of the asset. Absent preconfigured access tokens, when the user submits a real-time access request, the blockchain smart contract could send an acknowledgment or token access mechanism to the physical asset or user ewallet, such as a one-use QR code to open a rental car or hotel room. Blockchain technology offers the ability to reinvent identity authentication and secure access in ways that are much more granular, flexible, and oriented to real-time demand than are currently possible, elegantly integrating physical-world hardware technologies with digital Internet-based software technologies.[52]

Smart property transacted with blockchains is a completely new kind of concept. We are not used to having cryptographically defined property rights that are self-enforced by code. The code is self-enforced by the technical infrastructure in the sense that it is bound to operate based on the underlying code and cannot deviate. A property transfer specified in the code cannot but occur as encoded. Blockchain-based smart property thus contemplates the possibility of widespread decentralized trustless asset management systems as well as cryptographically activated assets. There could be widespread implications for the entire field of property law—or great simplifications in that property ownership can be recorded on the property itself:

Trustless lending

The trustless networks feature of blockchain technology is a key enabler in the context of smart property and smart contracts. Making property smart allows it to be traded with much less trust. This reduces fraud and mediation fees, but more importantly affords a much greater amount of trade to take place that otherwise would never have happened, because parties do not need to know and trust each other. For example, it makes it possible for strangers to lend you money over the Internet, taking your smart property as collateral, which should make lending more competitive and thus credit cheaper.[53] Further, there is the possibility that smart contracts executed in trustless networks could result in much less disputation. Contract disputes in the United States (44%) and United Kingdom (57%) account for the largest type of litigation, and might be avoided with more precision at the time of setting forth agreements, and with automated enforcement mechanisms.[54] Related to this, as cryptocurrency visionary and smart contracts legal theorist Nick Szabo points out, is the general problem of poor (i.e., irrational) human decision making, which might be improved with automated mechanisms like smart contracts.

Colored coins

One of the first implementations of smart property on the blockchain is colored coins (*http://coloredcoins.org/*). Certain Bitcoins are "colored" or "tagged" as corresponding to a particular asset or issuer via the transaction memo field in a Bitcoin transaction. The idea is similar to giving someone a dollar bill with an IOU for another property asset (e.g., a car) written on it. Thus, certain Bitcoins encode some other asset that can be securely transacted with the blockchain. This model still requires some trust—in this case, that the asset called out in the memo field will be deployed as agreed. Consequently, colored coins are intended for use within a certain community, serving as loyalty points or tokens to denote a range of physical and digital goods and services. The basic idea is that colored coins are Bitcoins marked with certain properties to reflect certain digital or physical assets so that more complex transactions can be carried out with the blockchain. The transactions could be asset exchange, and also the conduct of various activities within communities, such as voting, tipping, and commenting in forums.[55]

Smart Contracts

A general sense of blockchain-based smart contracts emerges from the smart property discussion. In the blockchain context, contracts or smart contracts mean blockchain transactions that go beyond simple buy/sell currency transactions, and may have more extensive instructions embedded into them. In a more formal definition, a contract is a method of using Bitcoin to form agreements with people via the blockchain. A contract in the traditional sense is an agreement between two or more parties to do or not do something in exchange for something else. Each party must trust the other party to fulfill its side of the obligation. Smart contracts feature the same kind of agreement to act or not act, but they remove the need for one type of trust between parties. This is because a smart contract is both defined by the code and executed (or enforced) by the code, automatically without discretion. In fact, three elements of smart contracts that make them distinct are autonomy, self-sufficiency, and decentralization. *Autonomy* means that after it is launched and running, a contract and its initiating agent need not be in further contact. Second, smart contracts might be *self-sufficient* in their ability to marshal resources—that is, raising funds by providing services or issuing equity, and spending them on needed resources, such as processing power or storage. Third, smart contracts are *decentralized* in that they do not subsist on a single centralized server; they are distributed and self-executing across network nodes.[56]

The classic example used to demonstrate smart contracts in the form of code executing automatically is a vending machine. Unlike a person, a vending machine behaves algorithmically; the same instruction set will be followed every time in every case. When you deposit money and make a selection, the item is released. There is no possibility of the machine not feeling like complying with the contract today, or only partially complying (as long as it is not broken). A smart contract similarly cannot help but execute the prespecified code. As Lessig reminds us, "code is law" in the sense that the code will execute no matter what. This could be good or bad depending on the situation; either way, it is a new kind of situation in society that will require a heavy accommodation period if blockchain-based smart contracts are to become widespread.

There are many considerations raised by smart contracts and systems of cryptographically activated assets with regard to whether we need a new body of law and regulation that distinguishes between technically binding code contracts and our more flexible legally binding human contracts.[57] Contract compliance or breach is at the discretion of human agents in a way that it is not with blockchain-based or any kind of code-based contracts. Further, smart contracts impact not just contract law, but more broadly the notion of the social contract within society. We need to determine and define what kinds of social contracts we would like with "code law," automatically and potentially unstoppably executing code. Because it could be nearly impossible to enforce smart contracts with law as currently enacted (for example, a decentralized code swatch running after the fact is difficult to control, regulate, or sue for damages), the legal framework is essentially pushed down to the level of the contract. The endpoint is not lawlessness and anarchy, but that legal frameworks become more granular and personalized to the situation. Parties agreeing to the contract could choose a legal framework to be incorporated into the code. There could be multiple known, vetted, "canned" legal frameworks, similar to Creative Commons licenses, such that users pick a legal framework as a feature of a smart contract. Thus, there could be a multiplicity of legal frameworks, just as there could be a multiplicity of currencies.

Contracts do not make anything possible that was previously impossible; rather, they allow common problems to be solved in a way that minimizes the need for trust. Minimal trust often makes things more convenient by taking human judgment out of the equation, thus allowing complete automation. An example of a basic smart contract on the blockchain is an inheritance gift that becomes available on either the grandchild's eighteenth birthday or the grandparent's day of death. A transaction can be created that sits on the blockchain and goes uninitiated until certain future events are triggered, either a certain time or event. To set up the first condition—the grandchild receiving the inheritance at age 18—the program sets the date on which to initiate the transaction, which includes checking if the transaction has already been executed. To set up the second condition, a program can be written that scans an online death registry database, prespecified online newspaper obituaries, or some other kind of information "oracle" to certify that the grandparent has died. When the smart contract confirms the death, it can automatically send the funds.[58] The Daniel Suarez science-fiction book *Daemon* implements exactly these kinds of smart contracts that are effected upon a character's death.

Another use case for smart contracts is setting up automatic payments for betting (like limit orders in financial markets). A program or smart contract can be written that releases a payment when a specific value of a certain exchange good is triggered or when something transpires in the real world (e.g., a news event of some sort, or the winner of a sports match). Smart contracts could also be deployed in pledge systems like Kickstarter. Individuals make online pledges that are encoded in a blockchain, and if the entrepreneur's fundraising goal is reached, only then will the Bitcoin funds be released from the investor wallets. No transaction is released until all funds are received. Further, the entrepreneur's budget, spending, and burn rate could be tracked by the subsequent outflow transactions from the blockchain address that received the fundraising.

Blockchain 2.0 Protocol Projects

There are many next-generation blockchain technology development projects that can be very loosely gathered under the header of Blockchain 2.0 protocol projects (Table 2-2), although this label is not perfect. The intent of Table 2-2 is to list some of the current high-profile projects, not to get into the descriptive details of how the projects differ technically or conceptually.

Table 2-2. Sample list of Blockchain 2.0 projects (extended from Piotr Piaseki, http://bit.ly/cr ypto_2_0_comp)

Bitcoin 2.0 project name and URL	Project description	Technical note
Ripple *https://ripple.com/*	Gateway, payment, exchange, remittance network; smart contract system: Codius	Separate blockchain
Counterparty *https://www.counterparty.co/*	Overlay protocol for currency issuance and exchange	Bitcoin blockchain overlay
Ethereum *http://ethereum.org/*	General-purpose Turing-complete cryptocurrency platform	Own blockchain, Ethereum virtual machine
Mastercoin *http://www.mastercoin.org/*	Financial derivatives	Bitcoin blockchain overlay
NXT *http://www.nxtcommunity.org/*	Altcoin mined with proof-of-stake consensus model	Bitcoin blockchain overlay
Open Transactions *http://opentransactions.org/*	Untraceable anonymous, no latency transactions	No blockchain; transactions library
BitShares *http://bitshares.org/*	Decentralized crypto-equity share exchange	Separate blockchain
Open Assets *https://github.com/OpenAssets*	Colored coin issuance and wallet	Bitcoin blockchain overlay
Colored Coins *http://coloredcoins.org/*	Bitcoin asset marking for digital/physical assets	Bitcoin blockchain overlay

Wallet Development Projects

Perhaps the primary category of applications being built atop blockchain protocols is wallets. Wallets are obviously a core infrastructural element for cryptocurrencies, because they are the mechanism for the secure holding and transfer of Bitcoin and any cryptographic asset. Table 2-3 lists some of the different wallet projects and companies in development, with their name and URL and the underlying platform upon which they are built.

Table 2-3. Sample list of cryptocurrency wallet projects

Project name	URL	Underlying infrastructure
Wallet projects		
ChromaWallet	*http://chromawallet.com/*	Open Assets
CoinSpark	*http://coinspark.org/*	Open Assets
Counterwallet	*https://counterwallet.io/*	Counterparty
Wallet companies		
Coinprism	*https://www.coinprism.com/*	Open Assets
Melotic	*https://www.melotic.com/*	Ability to trade curated digital assets (e.g., Storjcoin, LTBCoin) with Bitcoin
OneWallet	*https://www.onewallet.io*	Bitcoin marketplace and wallet

Blockchain Development Platforms and APIs

In addition to Blockchain 2.0 protocol projects, there are several developer platform companies and projects offering tools to facilitate application development. Blockchain.info (*https://blockchain.info/api*) has a number of APIs for working with its ewallet software (it's one of the largest ewallet providers) to make and receive payments and engage in other operations. Chain (*https://chain.com/*) has interfaces to make calls to the data available in full blockchain nodes, and standard information queries such as the Bitcoin balances by address and push notifications when there is activity with a certain address. Stellar (*https://www.stellar.org/*) is a *semidecentralized* (maintained by gateway institutions, not miners) public ledger platform and unified development environment (blockchain APIs, multisig APIs) linked to the Stripe payment network.[59] Related to Stellar are Block.io (*https://block.io*), Gem (*https://gem.co/*), and BlockCypher (*http://www.blockcypher.com/*), which have multisig wallet APIs.

More unified API development environments will be needed that include the many diverse and growing parts of the blockchain ecosystem (storage, file serving, messaging, wallet interactions, mobile payments, identity confirmation, and reputation). There is also an opportunity to link blockchain development environments out to other major segments like the machine-to-machine (M2M) communication and

Internet-of-Things (IoT) networks infrastructure for rapid application development. An example of an advanced integrated application of this kind envisioned for the farther future could be a smartwatch that can interact with smart-city traffic-sensor data to automatically reserve and pay for lane space with a Bitcoin-denominated smart contract.

Blockchain Ecosystem: Decentralized Storage, Communication, and Computation

There is a need for a decentralized ecosystem surrounding the blockchain itself for full-solution operations. The blockchain is the decentralized transaction ledger that is part of a larger computing infrastructure that must also include many other functions such as storage, communication, file serving, and archiving. Specific projects that are developing solutions for the distributed blockchain ecosystem include Storj for any sort of file storage (text, images, audio, multimedia); IPFS for file serving, link maintenance, and storage; and Maidsafe (*http://maidsafe.net/*) and Ethereum for storage, communication, and file serving. First, in terms of storage, perhaps the most obvious need is for secure, decentralized, off-chain storage for files such as an electronic medical record (EMR) or genome, or even any simple Microsoft Word document, which would not be packed into the 40-byte (40-character) OP_RETURN field used for transaction annotation (even in the case of Florincoin's 528-character annotation field). File storage could either be centralized (like Dropbox or Google Drive) or could be in the same decentralized architecture as the blockchain. The blockchain transaction that registers the asset can include a pointer and access method and privileges for the off-chain stored file.

Second, in the case of file serving, the IPFS project (*http://ipfs.io/*) has proposed an interesting technique for decentralized secure file serving. IPFS stands for *InterPlanetary File System*, which refers to the need for a global and permanently accessible filesystem to resolve the problem of broken website links to files, well beyond the context of blockchain technology for the overall functionality of the Internet. Here, BitTorrent peer-to-peer file-sharing technology has been merged with the tree and versioning functionality of Git (initially applied to software but "confirmable versioning" as a concept being more widely applicable to any digital asset). IPFS, then, is a global, versioned, peer-to-peer filesystem, a system for requesting and serving a file from any of the multiple places it might exist on the Web (versus having to rely on a central repository) per a hash (unique code) that confirms the file's integrity by checking that spam and viruses are not in the file.[60] IPFS is congruent with the Bitcoin technical architecture and ethos, rewarding file-sharing nodes with Filecoin (*http://filecoin.io/*).

Third, in the area of archiving, a full ecosystem would also necessarily include longevity provisioning and end-of-product-life planning for blockchains. It cannot be assumed that blockchains will exist over time, and their preservation and accessibility is not trivial. A blockchain archival system like the Internet Archive (*https://archive.org/*) and the Wayback Machine to store blockchains is needed. Not only must blockchain ledger transactions be preserved, but we also need a means of recovering and controlling previously recorded blockchain assets at later dates (that might have been hashed with proprietary algorithms) because it is likely that certain blockchains will go out of business. For example, it is great that someone established proof-of-existence of her will on the Bitcoin blockchain in 2014, but how can we know that the will can be rehashed and authenticated in 60 years when it needs to be verified? If blockchains are to become the lingua franca archival mechanism for the whole of a society's documents, longevity, preservation, and access mechanisms need to be built into the value chain explicitly. Further, the existence of these kinds of tools—those that archive out-of-use blockchains and consider the full product lifecycle of the blockchain—could help to spur mainstream adoption.

Ethereum: Turing-Complete Virtual Machine

Blockchain technology is bringing together concepts and operations from several fields, including computing, communications networks, cryptography, and artificial intelligence. In Satoshi Nakamoto's original plan, there were three steps, only two of which have been implemented in Bitcoin 1.0. These are the blockchain (the decentralized public transaction ledger) and the Bitcoin protocol (the transaction system to move value between parties without third-party interaction). This has been fine for the Blockchain 1.0 implementation of currency and payment transactions, but for the more complicated tier of Blockchain 2.0 applications such as the recording and transfer of more complex assets like smart property and smart contracts, we need the third step—a more robust scripting system—and ultimately, *Turing completeness* (the ability to run any coin, protocol, or blockchain). Nakamoto envisioned not just sending money from point A to point B, but having programmable money and a full feature set to enable it. One blockchain infrastructure project aiming to deliver a Turing-complete scripting language and Turing-complete platform is Ethereum.

Ethereum is a platform and a programming language for building and publishing distributed applications. More fundamentally, Ethereum is a foundational general-purpose cryptocurrency platform that is a Turing-complete virtual machine (meaning that it can run any coin, script, or cryptocurrency project). Rather than being a blockchain, or a protocol running over a blockchain, or a metaprotocol running over a protocol like other projects, Ethereum is a fundamental underlying infrastructure platform that can run all blockchains and protocols, rather like a unified universal development platform. Each full node in the Ethereum network runs the Ethereum Virtual Machine for seamless distributed program (smart contract) execution. Ethereum is the underlying blockchain-agnostic, protocol-agnostic platform for application development to write smart contracts that can call multiple other blockchains, protocols, and cryptocurrencies. Ethereum has its own distributed ecosystem, which is envisioned to include file serving, messaging, and reputation vouching. The first component is Swarm ("Ethereum-Swarm," not to be confused with the crowdfunding site Swarm) as a decentralized file-serving method. A second component is Whisper ("Ethereum-Whisper," also not to be confused with other similarly named projects), which is a peer-to-peer protocol for secret messaging and digital cryptography. A third component is a reputation system, a way to establish reputation and reduce risk between agents in trustless networks, possibly provided by TrustDavis,[61] or ideas developed in a hackathon project, Crypto Schwartz.[62]

Counterparty Re-creates Ethereum's Smart Contract Platform

In November 2014, Counterparty announced that it had ported the open source Ethereum programming language onto its own platform.[63] The implication was that Counterparty re-created Ethereum on the existing blockchain standard, Bitcoin, so that these kinds of smart contracts might be available now, without waiting for the launch (and mining operation) of Ethereum's own blockchain, expected in the first quarter of 2015 as of November 2014.

The announcement was a sign of the dynamism in the space and the rapid innovation that open source software enables (like most blockchain industry projects, both Ethereum and Counterparty's software is all open source). Any individual or any other project can freely examine and work with the code of other projects and bring it into their own implementations. This is the whole proposition of open source software. It means that good ideas can take seed more rapidly, become standardized through iteration, and be improved through the scrutiny and contributions of others. Ethereum and Counterparty both have deep visions for the future architecture of blockchain technology and decentralization, and establishing the infrastructural layers early in the process can help everyone progress to the next levels.[64] Given the functionality fungibility across some of the many protocols and platforms in the blockchain industry, perhaps the biggest question is what kinds of value-added services will be built atop these infrastructural layers; that is, what is the Netscape, Amazon, and Uber of the future?

Dapps, DAOs, DACs, and DASs: Increasingly Autonomous Smart Contracts

We can now see a progression trajectory. The first classes of blockchain applications are currency transactions; then all manner of financial transactions; then smart property, which instantiates all hard assets (house, car) and soft assets (IP) as digital assets; then government document registries, legal attestation, notary, and IP services; and finally, smart contracts that can invoke all of these digital asset types. Over time, smart contracts could become extremely complex and autonomous. Dapps, DAOs,

DACs, DASs, automatic markets, and tradenets are some of the more intricate concepts being envisioned for later-stage blockchain deployments. Keeping the description here at a summary level, the general idea is that with smart contracts (Blockchain 2.0; more complex transactions than those related to payments and currency transfer), there could be an increasing progression in the autonomy by which smart contracts operate. The simplest smart contract might be a bet between two parties about the maximum temperature tomorrow. Tomorrow, the contract could be automatically completed by a software program checking the official temperature reading (from a prespecified external source or oracle (in this example, perhaps Weather.com), and transferring the Bitcoin amount held in escrow from the loser to the winner's account.

Dapps

Dapps, DAOs, DACs, and DASs are abbreviated terms for decentralized applications, decentralized autonomous organizations, decentralized autonomous corporations, and decentralized autonomous societies, respectively. Essentially this group connotes a potential progression to increasingly complex and automated smart contracts that become more like self-contained entities, conducting preprogrammed and eventually self-programmed operations linked to a blockchain. In some sense the whole wave of Blockchain 2.0 protocols is Dapps (distributed applications), as is Blockchain 1.0 (the blockchain is a Dapp that maintains a public transaction ledger). Different parties have different definitions of what constitutes a Dapp. For example, Ethereum defines a smart contract/Dapp as a transaction protocol that executes the terms of a contract or group of contracts on a cryptographic blockchain.[65]

Our working definition of a Dapp is an application that runs on a network in a distributed fashion with participant information securely (and possibly pseudonymously) protected and operation execution decentralized across network nodes. Some current examples are listed in Table 2-4. There is OpenBazaar (a decentralized Craigslist), LaZooz (a decentralized Uber), Twister (a decentralized Twitter), Bitmessage (decentralized SMS), and Storj (decentralized file storage).

Table 2-4. Sample list of Dapps

Project name and URL	Activity	Centralized equivalent
OpenBazaar https://openbazaar.org/	Buy/sell items in local physical world	Craigslist
LaZooz http://lazooz.org/	Ridesharing, including Zooz, a proof-of-movement coin	Uber
Twister http://twister.net.co/	Social networking, peer-to-peer microblogging[66]	Twitter/Facebook
Gems http://getgems.org/	Social networking, token-based social messaging	Twitter/SMS

Project name and URL	Activity	Centralized equivalent
Bitmessage https://bitmessage.org	Secure messaging (individual or broadcast)	SMS services
Storj http://storj.io/	File storage	Dropbox
Swarm https://www.swarm.co/ Koinify https://koinify.com/ bitFlyer http://fundflyer.bitflyer.jp/	Cryptocurrency crowdfunding platforms	Kickstarter, Indiegogo venture capital funding

In a collaborative white paper, another group offers a stronger-form definition of a Dapp.[67] In their view, the Dapp must have three features. First, the application must be completely open source, operate autonomously with no entity controlling the majority of its tokens, and its data and records of operation must be cryptographically stored in a public, decentralized blockchain. Second, the application must generate tokens according to a standard algorithm or set of criteria and possibly distribute some or all of its tokens at the beginning of its operation. These tokens must be necessary for the use of the application, and any contribution from users should be rewarded by payment in the application's tokens. Third, the application may adapt its protocol in response to proposed improvements and market feedback, but all changes must be decided by majority consensus of its users. Overall, however, at present every blockchain project may have a slightly different idea of the exact technicalities of what the term *decentralized application* comprises.

DAOs and DACs

A DAO (decentralized autonomous organization) is a more complex form of a decentralized application. To become an organization more formally, a Dapp might adopt more complicated functionality such as a constitution, which would outline its governance publicly on the blockchain, and a mechanism for financing its operations such as issuing equity in a crowdfunding. DAOs/DACs (decentralized autonomous organizations/corporations) are a concept derived from artificial intelligence. Here, a decentralized network of autonomous agents perform tasks, which can be conceived in the model of a corporation running without any human involvement under the control of a set of business rules.[68] In a DAO/DAC, there are smart contracts as agents running on blockchains that execute ranges of prespecified or preapproved tasks based on events and changing conditions.[69] Not only would groups of smart contracts operating on the blockchain start to instantiate the model of an autonomous corporation, but the functions and operation of real physical-world businesses could be reconceived on the blockchain, as well. As Bitcoin currency transactions reinvent and make the remittances market more efficient, DAOs and DACs could do the same for businesses. A remittance operator might have many costs associated with physical plant and locational jurisdiction, and so, too, do businesses, with local jurisdictional compliance such as business licensing, registration, insurance, and taxation at many municipal and regulatory levels. Perhaps some of these functions could be reinvented in a more efficient way or eliminated when moved to the blockchain, and every business could be truly global. Cloud-based, blockchain-based autonomous business entities running via smart contract could then electronically contract with compliance entities like governments to self-register in any jurisdictions in which they wanted to operate. Every business could be a general universal business first, and a jurisdictional business later when better decisions can be made about jurisdictions. The same could be true for individuals as general humans first, and citizens on demand later.

One example of the DAO/DAC concept in terms of automated smart contract operation is Storj. As previously mentioned, Storj is a decentralized cloud storage platform that completed a $461,802 crowdfunding in August 2014.[70] Storj uses the Bitcoin blockchain technology and peer-to-peer protocols to provide secure, private, and encrypted cloud storage. There are two apps, DriveShare and MetaDisk, which respectively enable users to rent out their unused hard disk space and store their files on the Storj network. Purported methods for safely sharing unused hard disk space have been developed by other community computing models like Folding@Home and BOINC, whose software is used by SETI@Home. Of course, as with any distributed project that involves opening your computer to others' use, *caveat emptor* applies, and participants in Storj or any similar project should satisfactorily inform themselves of the security details. Storj's altcoin token, Storjcoin X (SJCX), is a cryptocurrency that runs on the Counterparty protocol. The currency is used to purchase space on the Storj network via Metadisk and compensate network DriveShare storage providers. Storj is seen as a decentralized alternative to storage providers like Dropbox or Google; the company estimates that customers overpay for data storage by a factor of 10 to 100, and that blockchain methods could provide cheaper, more secure, and decentralized data storage.[71]

DASs and Self-Bootstrapped Organizations

Eventually there could be DASs (decentralized autonomous societies)—essentially fleets of smart contracts, or entire ecosystems of Dapps, DAOs, and DACs operating autonomously. An interesting concept related to intellectual property and new ideas is the "self-bootstrapped organization."[72] This is a new business idea arising from the blockchain or via a person, in which the project idea spins out to become a standalone entity with some standardized smart-contract, self-bootstrapping software to crowdfund itself based on a mission statement; operate; pay dividends or other remuneration back to crowdfunding investors; receive feedback (automated or orchestrated) through blockchain prediction markets and decentralized blockchain voting; and eventually dissolve or have periodic confirmation-of-instantiation votes (similar to business relationship contracts evergreening or calling for periodic reevaluations). Automatic dissolution or reevaluation clauses could be critical in avoiding situations like those described in Daniel Suarez's science-fiction books *Daemon* and *Freedom*, in which the world economy ends up radically transformed by the smart-contract type agents inexorably following their programmed code.

Automatic Markets and Tradenets

An automatic market is the idea that unitized, packetized, quantized resources (initially like electricity, gas, bandwidth, and in the deeply speculative future, units of synaptic potentiation in brains) are automatically transacted based on dynamically evolving conditions and preprogrammed user profiles, permissions, and bidding functions.[73] Algorithmic stock market trading and real-time bidding (RTB) advertising networks (*http://bit.ly/rtb_ad_networks*) are the closest existing examples of automatic markets. In the future, automatic markets could be applied in the sense of having limit orders and program trading for physical-world resource allocation. Truly smart grids (e.g., energy, highway, and traffic grids) could have automatic bidding functions on both the cost and revenue side of their operations—for both inputs (resources) and outputs (customers) and participation in automatic clearing mechanisms. A related concept is tradenets: in the future there could be self-operating, self-owned assets like a self-driving, self-owning car.[74] Self-directing assets would employ themselves for trade based on being continuously connected to information from the Internet to be able to assess dynamic demand for themselves, contract with potential customers like Uber does now, hedge against oil price increases with their own predictive resource planning, and ultimately self-retire at the end of their useful life—in short, executing all aspects of autonomous self-operation. Tradenets could even have embedded, automatically executing smart contracts to trigger the building of new transportation pods based on signals of population growth, demand, and business plan validity.

The Blockchain as a Path to Artificial Intelligence

We should think of smart contracts as applications that can themselves be decentralized, autonomous, and pseudonymously running on the blockchain. Thus, the blockchain could be one potential path to artificial intelligence (AI) in the sense that smart-contract platforms are being designed to run at graduated stages of increasing automation, autonomy, and complexity. With Dapps, DAOs, DACs, and DASs, there could be many interesting new kinds of emergent and complex AI-like behavior. One possible path is bringing existing non-AI and non-blockchain rule-based systems onto the blockchain to further automate and empower their operations. This could include systems like chaining together simple if-this-then-that (or IFTTT (*https:// ifttt.com/*)) behavior and the open source Huginn platform (*https://github.com/ cantino/huginn*) for building agents that monitor situations and act on your behalf. A second possible path is implementing programmatic ideas from AI research fields such as Wolfram's cellular automata, Conway's Game of Life, Dorigo's Ant Colony Optimization and Swarm Intelligence, Andy Clark's embodied cognitive robots, and other general agent-based systems.

CHAPTER 3

Blockchain 3.0: Justice Applications Beyond Currency, Economics, and Markets

Blockchain Technology Is a New and Highly Effective Model for Organizing Activity

Not only is there the possibility that blockchain technology could reinvent every category of monetary markets, payments, financial services, and economics, but it might also offer similar reconfiguration possibilities to all industries, and even more broadly, to nearly all areas of human endeavor. The blockchain is fundamentally a new paradigm for organizing activity with less friction and more efficiency, and at much greater scale than current paradigms. It is not just that blockchain technology is decentralized and that decentralization as a general model can work well now because there is a liquid enough underlying network with the Web interconnecting all humans, including for disintermediated transactions: blockchain technology affords a universal and global scope and scale that was previously impossible. This can be true for resource allocation, in particular to allow for increasingly automated resource allocation of physical-world assets and also human assets. Blockchain technology facilitates the coordination and acknowledgment of all manner of human interaction, facilitating a higher order of collaboration and possibly paving the way for human/machine interaction. Perhaps all modes of human activity could be coordinated with blockchain technology to some degree, or at a minimum reinvented with blockchain concepts. Further, blockchain technology is not just a better organizational model functionally, practically, and quantitatively; by requiring consensus to operate, the model could also have greater liberty, equality, and empowerment qualitatively. Thus, the blockchain is a complete solution that integrates both extrinsic and intrinsic and qualitative and quantitative benefits.

Extensibility of Blockchain Technology Concepts

Blockchain technology can potentially unleash an important element of creativity and invention in anyone who encounters the concepts in a broad and general way. This is in the sense that it is necessary to understand the new ideas separately and together. These include concepts such as public-key and private-key cryptography, peer-to-peer file sharing, distributed computing, network models, pseudonymity, blockchain ledgers, cryptocurrency protocols, and cryptocurrency. This calls into question what might have seemed to be established definitions of traditional parameters of the modern world like currency, economics, trust, value, and exchange. It is a requirement and twenty-first-century skill set to understand these concepts in order to operate in the blockchain technology environment. When you understand the concepts involved, not only is it possible to innovate blockchain-related solutions, but further, the concepts are portable to other contexts. This extensibility of blockchain-related concepts may be the source of the greatest impact of blockchain technology as human agents understand these concepts and deploy them in every venue they can imagine. The Internet was a similar example of universality in application and extensibility of the core technology concept; it meant that everything could be done in a new way— quicker, with greater reach, in real time, on demand, via worldwide broadcast, at lower cost. Blockchain technology is rich with new concepts that could become part of the standard intellectual vernacular and toolkit.

Fundamental Economic Principles: Discovery, Value Attribution, and Exchange

One broad way of thinking about the use of blockchain concepts is applying them beyond the original context to see ways in which everything is like an economy, a market, and a currency—and equally important, how everything is *not* like an economy. This is a mindset that requires recognizing the fundamental properties of economics and markets in real-life situations. Blockchain technology helps elucidate that everything we see and experience, every system in life, is economics to some degree: a system for allocating resources. Furthermore, systems and interactions are economics in that they are a matter of awareness and discovery, value attribution, and potential interaction and exchange, and may include a mechanism for this exchange like a currency or token, or even a simple exchange of force, energy, or concentration (as in biological systems). This same basic economic structure could be said to exist universally, whether in a collaborative work team or at a farmers' market. The quantized structure of blockchain technology in the form of ledger transaction-level tracking could mean higher-resolution activity tracking, several orders of magnitude more detailed and extensive than we are accustomed to at present, a time at which we are still grateful for SKU-level tracking on a bill of materials.

Blockchain tracking could mean that all contributions to a system by all involved parties, no matter how minute, can be assessed and attributed in a seamless, automated way, for later roll-up to the macro level—or not, because some community value systems might dictate not having user contributions explicitly tracked. The ethos and morality of tracking is a separate and interesting social-science topic to explore in the blockchain studies research agenda more generally. However, one way that the blockchain-based capacity for tracking could work is in the form of a "GitHub + Bitcoin" concept, for example, that tracks code contributions line by line over all revisions of a software code corpus over time. This is important, because economically savvy rational agents participating in the system (i.e., currently humans) want to assess the contributions they and others have made, and have these contributions tracked and acknowledged for remuneration, reputation, status garnering, and other rewards.

Blockchain Technology Could Be Used in the Administration of All Quanta

What the blockchain could facilitate in an automated computational way is one universal, seamless model for the coordinated activity of near-infinite numbers of transactions, a universal transaction system on an order never before imagined for human activity. In some sense, blockchain technology could be a supercomputer for reality. Any and all phenomena that can be quantized (defined in discrete units or packages) can be denoted this way and encoded and transacted in an automated fashion on the blockchain. Blockchain venture capitalist David Johnston's summary and prognostication of this dynamic is that anything that can be decentralized will be, showing his belief in the inherent efficiency and benefit or superiority of the blockchain model. Decentralization is "where water goes," where water flows naturally, along the way of least resistance and least effort. The blockchain could be an Occam's razor, the most efficient, direct, and natural means of coordinating all human and machine activity; it is a natural efficiency process.

Blockchain Layer Could Facilitate Big Data's Predictive Task Automation

As big data allows the predictive modeling of more and more processes of reality, blockchain technology could help turn prediction into action. Blockchain technology could be joined with big data, layered onto the reactive-to-predictive transformation that is slowly under way in big-data science to allow the automated operation of large areas of tasks through smart contracts and economics. Big data's predictive analysis could dovetail perfectly with the automatic execution of smart contracts. We could accomplish this specifically by adding blockchain technology as the embedded economic payments layer and the tool for the administration of quanta, implemented through automated smart contracts, Dapps, DAOs, and DACs. The automated operation of huge classes of tasks could relieve humans because the tasks would instead be handled by a universal, decentralized, globally distributed computing system. We thought big data was big, but the potential quantization and tracking and administration of all classes of activity and reality via blockchain technology at both lower and higher resolutions hints at the next orders-of-magnitude progression up from the current big-data era that is itself still developing.

Distributed Censorship-Resistant Organizational Models

The primary argument for Blockchain 1.0 and 2.0 transactions is the economic efficiency and cost savings afforded by trustless interaction in decentralized network models, but freedom and empowerment are also important dimensions of the blockchain. Decentralized models can be especially effective at promoting freedom and economic transfer in countries with restrictive political regimes and capital controls. Freedom is available in the sense of pseudonymous transactions outside of the visibility, tracking, and regulatory purview of local governments. This can be a significant issue for citizens in emerging markets where local capital controls, government regulations, and overly restrictive economic environments make it much harder to engage in a variety of standard activities, including starting new businesses. State economic controls, together with a lack of trust in fiat currency, have been driving a lot of interest in cryptocurrencies.

The freedom attribute associated with blockchain technologies becomes more pronounced in Blockchain 3.0, the next category of application beyond currency and market transactions. Through its global decentralized nature, blockchain technology has the potential ability to circumvent the current limitations of geographic jurisdictions. There is an argument that blockchain technology can more equitably address issues related to freedom, jurisdiction, censorship, and regulation, perhaps in ways that nation-state models and international diplomacy efforts regarding human rights cannot. Irrespective of supporting the legitimacy of nation-states, there is a scale and jurisdiction acknowledgment and argument that certain operations are transnational and are more effectively administered, coordinated, monitored, and reviewed at a higher organizational level such as that of a World Trade Organization.

The idea is to uplift transnational organizations from the limitations of geography-based, nation-state jurisdiction to a truly global cloud. The first point is that transnational organizations need transnational governance structures. The reach, accessibility, and transparency of blockchain technology could be an effective transnational governance structure. Blockchain governance is more congruent with the character and needs of transnational organizations than nation-state governance. The second point is that not only is the transnational governance provided by the blockchain more effective, it is fairer. There is potentially more equality, justice, and freedom available to organizations and their participants in a decentralized, cloud-based model. This is provided by the blockchain's immutable public record, transparency, access, and reach. Anyone worldwide could look up and confirm the activities of transnational organizations on the blockchain. Thus, the blockchain is a global system of checks and balances that creates trust among all parties. This is precisely the sort of core infrastructural element that could allow humanity to scale to orders-of-magnitude larger progress with truly global organizations and coordination mechanisms.

One activity for which this could make sense is the administration of the Internet. Internet administration organizations have a transnational purview but are based in nation-state localities. An example is ICANN, the Internet Corporation for Assigned Names and Numbers. ICANN manages Internet protocol numbers and namespaces, coordinating the translation of *www.example.com* to the numeric IP address 93.184.216.119 for connection across the Internet.

Blockchain technology simultaneously highlights the issue of the appropriate administration of transnational public goods and presents a solution. Wikipedia is a similar transnational public good that is currently subject to a local jurisdiction that could impose on the organization an artificial or biased agenda. It is possible that blockchain mechanisms might be the most efficient and equitable models for administering all transnational public goods, particularly due to their participative, democratic, and distributed nature.

A notable case in which jurisdictional nation-state entities were able to effect centralized and biased control is WikiLeaks. In the Edward Snowden whistle-blowing case in 2010, individuals were trying to make financial contributions in support of the WikiLeaks organization but, strongarmed by centralized government agendas, credit card payment networks and PayPal, refused to accept such contributions, and WikiLeaks was effectively embargoed.[75] Bitcoin contributions, had they been possible at the time, would have been direct, and possibly produced a different outcome. The Electronic Freedom Foundation (EFF), a nonprofit organization that supports personal freedoms, and other related organizations are similarly located in jurisdictional locations at present, which could always mean the operation of curtailed agendas if authorities were to exercise influence over the organization and individuals involved.

Namecoin: Decentralized Domain Name System

One of the first noncurrency uses of blockchain technology was to prevent Internet censorship with Namecoin (*https://wiki.namecoin.info*), an altcoin that can be used to verify Domain Name System (DNS) registrations. Namecoin is an alternative DNS that is transnational and cannot be controlled by any government or corporation. The benefit of a decentralized DNS is that it makes it possible for anyone worldwide who might be otherwise suppressed or censored to publish information freely in the Internet.

Just as Bitcoin is a decentralized currency that cannot be shut down, Namecoin is the basis for a decentralized DNS (i.e., web URLs).[76] The idea is that URLs permanently embedded in the blockchain would be resistant to the government seizing of domains. The censorship issue is that in a URL such as *google.com*, centralized authorities control the top-level domain, the *.com* portion (the United States controls *.com* URLs), and therefore can potentially seize and redirect the URL. Centralized authorities control all top-level domains; for example, China controls all *.cn* domains. Therefore, a decentralized DNS means that top-level domains can exist that are not controlled by anyone, and they have DNS lookup tables shared on a peer-to-peer network. As long as there are volunteers running the decentralized DNS server software, alternative domains registered in this system can be accessed. Authorities cannot impose rules to affect the operation of a well-designed and executed global peer-to-peer top-level domain. The same Bitcoin structure is used in the implementation of a separate blockchain and coin, Namecoin, for decentralized DNS.

Namecoin is not at present intended for the registration of all domains, but as a free speech mechanism for domains that might be sensitive to censorship (for example, in countries with limited political freedom). The top-level domain for Namecoin is *.bit*. Interested parties register *.bit* domains with Namecoin. The actions necessary to register a new domain or to update an existing one are built in to the Namecoin protocol, based on transaction type—for example, the "name_new" transaction at a cost of 0.01 NMC (Namecoin is convertible in/out of Bitcoin). Domains can be registered directly with the Namecoin system or via a registration service like *https://dotbit.me/*.

Because the top-level domain *.bit* is outside the traditional operation of the Internet, to facilitate viewing *.bit* websites, there are *.bit* proxy servers to handle DNS requests in a browser (*http://bit.ly/browsing_bit*), as well as Firefox (*http://www.meowbit.com/*) and Chrome extensions (*http://bit.ly/dot_bit_ext*). According to the Bitcoin Contact website (*http://namecoin.bitcoin-contact.org/*) as of October 2014, there are 178,397 *.bit* domains registered, including, for example, *wikileaks.bit*. The key point is that *.bit* domains are a free-speech mechanism, because now having the ability to view *.bit* websites means attempts to silence those with a legitimate message will have less of a chance of succeeding. Just as there are benefits to having decentralized currency transactions, there are benefits to having many other kinds of decentralized transactions.

Challenges and Other Decentralized DNS Services

Technical issues were found with the Namecoin implementation that left *.bit* domains vulnerable to takeover (a bug that made it possible to update values if the transaction input name matched the transaction output name, as well as new registrations to be overridden).[77] Developers have been remedying these issues. Other critics (as with Bitcoin in general) point out how the key features of decentralized DNS services (cheap and anonymous domain name creation, and a system that places domain names out of the reach of central authorities) enable bad players and illegality.[78] However, an industry white paper counters these claims with examples of using the public traceability feature of the blockchain ledger to apprehend criminals, and points out that there are many legitimate uses of this technology.[79]

Meanwhile, other decentralized name services are in development, such as a similar .P2P decentralized top-level domain (*http://dotp2p.io/*) from BitShares. The project points out how the decentralized DNS model eliminates the certificate authority as the third-party intermediary (which can leave URLs vulnerable to attack), and that a blockchain model can also be more secure because you lose control of your domain only if you share the private key.[80] DotP2P has other features to improve DNS registry, such as auction-like price discovery to counter domain-name squatting. Related to decentralized DNS services is digital identity confirmation services; in October 2014, BitShares launched the KeyID service toward this end. KeyID (*http://keyid.info/*), rebranded from Keyhotee, provides an identification and email system on a decentralized blockchain for secure messaging and for secure authentication.[81]

Freedom of Speech/Anti-Censorship Applications: Alexandria and Ostel

Alexandria is one example of a blockchain-based freedom-of-speech-promoting project. It aims to create an unalterable historical record by encoding Twitter feeds to a blockchain. Any tweets mentioning certain prespecified keywords (like *Ukraine* or *ebola*) are encoded into the Alexandria blockchain using Florincoin (*http://florincoin.org/*), a cryptocurrency based on Bitcoin and Litecoin with quick transaction processing (40 seconds) and a longer memo annotation field (conceptually: Memocoin). This method captures tweets that might be censored out later by takedown requests.[82] Florincoin's key enabling feature for this is transaction comments, a 528-character field for the recording of both metadata and tweet content.[83] The expanded commenting functionality could be used more broadly for many kinds of blockchain applications, such as providing metadata and secure pointers to genomic sequences or X-ray files. Another freedom-oriented application is Ostel's (*https://ostel.co/*) free encrypted Voice over IP (VoIP) telephony service, because the United States National Security Agency (NSA) can listen in on other services like Skype.[84] Ostel is a nice example of David Brin's bottom-up souveillance counterweight[85] to top-down NSA surveillance (of both traditional telephone calls and Skype[86]).

Decentralized DNS Functionality Beyond Free Speech: Digital Identity

Beyond its genesis motivation to enable free speech and provide a countermeasure to the centralized control of the Internet, there are other important uses of decentralized DNS functionality in the developing Blockchain 3.0 ecosystem. The blockchain is allowing a rethinking and decentralization of all Internet network operations—for example, DNS services (Namecoin, DotP2P), digital identity (KeyID, and OneName and BitID, which are discussed shortly), and network traffic communications (Open-Libernet.org, an open mesh network communications protocol).

One challenge related to Bitcoin, the Internet, and network communications more generally is Zooko's Triangle (*http://bit.ly/zookos_triangle*). This is the problem encountered in any system that gives names to participants in a network protocol: how to make identifiers such as a URL or a person's handle (e.g., DeMirage99) simultaneously secure, decentralized, and human-usable (i.e., not in the form of a 32-character alphanumeric string).[87] Innovations and maturity in blockchain technology require having solutions to the Zooko's Triangle challenge. Namecoin functionality might offer such a solution. Namecoin is used to store URLs, but it can store any information. The core functionality of Namecoin is that it is a name/value store system. Therefore, just as Bitcoin has uses beyond currency, Namecoin has uses beyond DNS for storing information more generally. Using the nondomain namespaces of Namecoin, we can store information that would otherwise be hard to securely or conveniently exchange. A prime application for this is a resolution to Zooko's Triangle, allowing continuously available Internet-based digital identity confirmation of a public key (a 32-character alphanumeric string) with a human-usable handle (DeMirage99) as digital identity services like OneName and BitID allow.

Digital Identity Verification

OneName (*https://www.onename.io/*) and BitID (*http://bitid.bitcoin.blue/*) are examples of blockchain-based digital identity services. They confirm an individual's identity to a website. Decentralized digital verification services take advantage of the fact that all Bitcoin users have a personal wallet, and therefore a wallet address. This could speed access to all aspects of websites, simultaneously improving user experience, anonymity, and security. It can also facilitate ecommerce because customers using Bitcoin-address login are already enabled for purchase.

On the surface, OneName is an elegant Bitcoin-facilitating utility, but in the background, it is a more sophisticated decentralized digital identity verification system that could be extensible beyond its initial use case. OneName helps solve the problem that 27- through 34-character Bitcoin addresses are (at the expense of being cryptographically sound) cumbersome for human users. Some other Bitcoin wallet services and exchanges, like Coinbase, have allowed Bitcoin to be sent to email addresses for some time. The OneName service is a more secure solution. With OneName, users can set up a more practical name (like a social media handle) to use for Bitcoin transactions. After a user is registered with OneName, asking for payment is as easy as adding a plus sign to your username (for example, +DeMirage99). OneName is an open source protocol built on the Namecoin protocol that puts users in charge of their digital identity verification, rather than allowing centralized social media sites like Facebook, LinkedIn, and Twitter to be the de facto identity verification platform, given that many websites have opted to authenticate users with social media APIs.[88]

A similar project is BitID, which allows users to log in to websites with their Bitcoin address. Instead of "Login with Facebook," you can "Connect with Bitcoin" (your Bitcoin address). BitID is a decentralized authentication protocol that takes advantage of Bitcoin wallets as a form of identification and QR codes for service or platform access points. It enables users to access an online account by verifying themselves with their wallet address and uses a mobile device as the private-key authenticator.[89]

Another proposed digital identity verification business is Bithandle (*http://www.hack athon.io/bithandle*), which was developed as a hackathon project. Bithandle offers short-handle registration, verification, and ecommerce service. As with Onename and BitID, users can register an easy-to-use handle—for instance, "Coinmaster"— that is linked to a wallet address via a public or private real-life identity check and a Bitcoin blockchain transaction. The service offers ongoing real-time digital identity verification and one-click auto-enabled ecommerce per "Login with Bitcoin" website access. An obvious problem with the mainstream adoption of Bitcoin is the unwieldy 32-character Bitcoin address, or QR code, needed to send and receive funds. Instead, Bithandle gives users the ability to link a short handle to a Bitcoin address, which is confirmed initially with real-life identity and looked up in the blockchain on demand at any future moment. Real-time digital identity verification services could be quite crucial; already the worldwide market size for identity authentication and verification is $11 billion annually.[90]

Specifically, how Bithandle works is that in the digital identity registration process, participants register a Bitcoin username, an easy-to-use handle that can then be used to "Login with Bitcoin" to websites. As mentioned, this is similar to the ability to access websites by "Login with Facebook" or "Login with Twitter" but automatically connects to a user's Bitcoin address for proof of identity. When a user sets up a Bithandle, his real-life identity is confirmed with Facebook, Twitter, LinkedIn, or other services, and this can be posted publically (like OneName) or not (as OneName does not allow), with the user's Bithandle.

Later, for real-time digital identity verification, "Logging in with Bitcoin" means that a Bithandle is already connected to a Bitcoin address, which securely facilitates ecommerce without the user having to register an account and provide personal identity and financial details. Bithandle thus helps streamline user interactions with websites in several ways. First, websites do not have to maintain user account registries ("honeypot" risks for hacking). Second, every user "Logging in with Bitcoin" is automatically enabled for one-click ecommerce purchases. Third, the Bithandle service can provide real-time blockchain lookups to confirm user digital identity at any future time on demand—for example, to reauthorize a user for subsequent purchases.

Blockchain Neutrality

Cryptography experts and blockchain developers and architects point out the importance of designing the blockchain industry with some of the same principles that have become baked in to the Internet structure over time, like neutrality. In the case of the Internet, *net neutrality* is the principle that Internet service providers should enable access to all content and applications regardless of the source and without favoring or blocking particular products or websites. The concept is similar for cryptocurrencies: *Bitcoin neutrality* means the ability for all persons everywhere to be able to easily adopt Bitcoin. This means that anyone can start using Bitcoin, in any and every culture, language, religion, and geography, political system, and economic regime.[91] Bitcoin is just a currency; it can be used within any kind of existing political, economic, or religious system. For example, the Islamic Bank of Bitcoin is investigating ways to conduct Sharia-compliant banking with Bitcoin.[92] A key point of Bitcoin neutrality is that the real target market for whom Bitcoin could be most useful is the "unbanked," individuals who do not have access to traditional banking services for any number of reasons, estimated at 53 percent of the worldwide population.[93] Even in the United States, 7.7 percent of households are forecast to be unbanked or underbanked.[94]

Bitcoin neutrality means access for the unbanked and underbanked, which requires Bitcoin solutions that apply in all low-tech environments, with features like SMS payment, paper wallets, and batched blockchain transactions. Having neutrality-oriented, easy-to-use solutions (the "Twitter of emerging market Bitcoin") for Bitcoin could trigger extremely fast uptake in underbanked markets, continuing the trend of 31 percent of Kenya's GDP being spent through mobile phones.[95] There are different SMS Bitcoin wallets and delivery mechanisms (like 37Coins (*https://www.37coins.com/*)[96] and Coinapult (*https://coinapult.com/*), and projects like Kipochi (*https://www.kipochi.com/*)[97] that are integrated with commonly used emerging-markets mobile finance platforms like M-Pesa. A similar project is a mobile crypto-wallet app, Saldo.mx, which uses the Ripple open source protocol for clearing, and links people living in the United States and Latin America for the remote payment of bills, insurance, airtime, credit, and products.

Digital Divide of Bitcoin

The term *digital divide* has typically referred to the gap between those who have access to certain technologies and those who do not. In the case of cryptocurrencies, if they are applied with the principles of neutrality, everyone worldwide might start to have access. Thus, alternative currencies could be a helpful tool for bridging the digital divide. However, there is another tier of digital divide beyond access: know-how. A new digital divide could arise (and arguably already has in some sense) between those who know how to operate securely on the Internet and those who do not. The principles of neutrality should be extended such that appropriate mainstream tools make it

---

possible for anyone to operate anonymously (or rather pseudonymously), privately, and securely in all of their web-based interactions and transactions.

Digital Art: Blockchain Attestation Services (Notary, Intellectual Property Protection)

Digital art is another arena in which blockchain cryptography can provide a paradigm-shifting improvement (it's also a good opportunity to discuss hashing and timestamping, important concepts for the rest of the book). The term *digital art* refers to intellectual property (IP) very generally, not just online artworks. *Art* is connoted in the patenting sense, meaning "owned IP." As we've discussed, in the context of digital asset proof and protection, identity can be seen as just one application, although one that might require more extensive specialty features. Whereas digital identity relies on users having a Bitcoin wallet address, digital asset proof in the context of attestation services relies on the blockchain functionality of hashing and timestamping. Attestation services (declaring something to be true, such as asset ownership) are referred to as digital art. The main use of the term *digital art* in the blockchain industry is to refer to using the blockchain to register any form of IP (entirely digital or representing something in the physical world) or conduct attestation services more generally, such as contract notarization. The term is also used in the blockchain industry to mean online graphics, images photographs, or digitally created artworks that are digital assets, and thus IP to protect.

Hashing Plus Timestamping

For attestation services, blockchain technology brings together two key functions: hashing and secure timestamping. Hashing is running a computing algorithm over any content file (a document, a genome file, a GIF file, a video, etc.), the result of which is a compressed string of alphanumeric characters that cannot be back-computed into the original content. For example, every human genome file could be turned into a 64-character hash string as a unique and private identifier for that content.[98] The hash represents the exact content of original file. Anytime the content needs to be reconfirmed, the same hash algorithm is run over the file, and the hash signature will be the same if the file has not changed. The hash is short enough to be included as text in a blockchain transaction, which thus provides the secure time-stamping function of when a specific attestation transaction occurred. Via the hash, the original file content has essentially been encoded into the blockchain. The blockchain can serve as a document registry.

The key idea is using cryptographic hashes as a form of asset verification and attestation, the importance of which could be extremely significant. Blockchain hash functionality could be a key function for the operation of the whole of society, using the blockchain to prove the existence and exact contents of any document or other digital asset at a certain time. Further, the blockchain attestation functionality of hashing-plus-timestamping supports the idea of the blockchain as a new class of information technology.

Blockchain attestation services more generally comprise all manner of services related to document filing, storage, and registry; notary services (validation); and IP protection. As articulated, these functions take advantage of the blockchain's ability to use cryptographic hashes as a permanent and public way to record and store information, and also to find it later with a block explorer and the blockchain address pointer from the blockchain as a universal central repository. The core functionality is the ability to verify a digital asset via a public general ledger.

There are several blockchain-based attestation services in different stages of development or proof of concept, such as Proof of Existence, Virtual Notary, Bitnotar, Chronobit, and Pavilion.io. The specifics of how they might be different or similar are emerging, and there is presumably a lot of functionality fungibility in that any of the services can simply hash a generic file of any type. The first and longest-standing service, Proof of Existence, is described in detail next.

Proof of Existence

One of the first services to offer blockchain attestation is Proof of Existence (*http://www.proofofexistence.com/*). People can use the web-based service to hash things such as art or software to prove authorship of the works.[99] Founder Manuel Aráoz had the idea of proving a document's integrity by using a cryptographic hash, but the problem was not knowing when the document was created, until the blockchain could add a trusted timestamping mechanism.[100] Proof of Existence demonstrates document ownership without revealing the information it contains, and it provides proof that a document was authored at a particular time. Figure 3-1 shows a screenshot from the scrolling list of newly registered digital assets with the Proof of Existence service.

Proof of Existence	Prove	About	API	Contact	

Last documents registered:

	Document Digest	Timestamp
	57df41a5b47a90ffba887fbd08d02ed00c271c5b7a97ed5a12fd462ab3ce8424	2014-10-31 04:04:21
✓	8d1ce7d930d1c17ff9fd0bc3c75f35d727267072ce53bfb019adbf9e0a6f575c	2014-10-31 03:55:49
✓	e249cacaa5bfd7ac2b1d10a63043d92ee3d332811c233db1f76642c54004303b	2014-10-31 03:34:53
✓	503cba6a57c426fd95d99a7efc884532c265efda425c3f45a7f7be7906b6a2e4	2014-10-31 02:29:00
	9119458b7e28933d71cc96327f7bd80ef84efd89b558825c27d2ebe8c265d30e	2014-10-31 01:06:54

Figure 3-1. "Last documents registered" digest from Proof of Existence

With this tool, the blockchain can be used to prove the existence and exact contents of a document or other digital asset at a certain time (a revolutionary capability). Providing timestamped data in an unalterable state while maintaining confidentiality is perfect for a wide range of legal and civic applications. Attorneys, clients, and public administrators could use the Proof of Existence blockchain functionality to prove the existence of many documents including wills, deeds, powers of attorney, health care directives, promissory notes, the satisfaction of a promissory note, and so on without disclosing the contents of the document. With the blockchain timestamp feature, users can prove that a document (like a will) they will be presenting to a court in the future is the same unaltered document that was presented to the blockchain at a prior point in time. These kinds of attestation services can be used for any kind of documents and digital assets. Developers, for example, can use the service to create unique hashes for each version of code that they create and later verify versions of their code, inventors can prove they had an idea at a certain time, and authors can protect their works.

The proof-of-existence function works in this way: first, you present your document (or any file) to the service website (*http://www.proofofexistence.com/*); you're then prompted to "click or drag and drop your document here." The site does not upload or copy the content of the document but instead (on the client side) converts the contents to a cryptographic digest or hash. Algorithms create a digest, or a cryptographic string that is representative of a piece of data; the digest created by a hash function is based on the characteristics of a document. No two digests are the same, unless the data used to compute the digests is the same. Thus, the hash represents the exact contents of the document presented. The cryptographic hash of the document is inserted into a transaction, and when the transaction is mined into a block, the block timestamp becomes the document's timestamp, and via the hash the document's content has essentially been encoded into the blockchain. When the same document is presented again, the same marker will be created and therefore provide verification that the documents are the same. If, however, the document has changed in any way, the new marker will not match the previous marker. This is how the system verifies the document.[101]

One benefit of attestation services is how efficiently they make use of the blockchain. Original documents are not stored on the blockchain, just their hash is stored, which is accessible by private key. Whenever a proof of existence needs to be confirmed, if the recomputed hash is the same as the original hash registered in the blockchain, the document can be verified as unchanged. The hash does not need to (and cannot) translate back into the document (hashes are only one-way; their security feature makes back-computation impossible). The retrieval phase of proof-of-existence functionality can be thought of as a "content verification service." Regarding longevity, the crucial part is having the private key to the digital asset (the hash) that is registered on the blockchain. This does mean trusting that whichever blockchain used will be available in the future; thus, it would be good to select an attestation service that uses a standard blockchain like the Bitcoin blockchain.

Limitations

Admittedly there are some limitations to hashing-plus-timestamping blockchain attestation services. First, a blockchain is not required for timestamping, because other third-party services provide this for free, whereas a small transaction fee (to compensate miners) is required to post a digital asset attestation to the blockchain. Also, blockchain transaction confirmations are not immediate; the time the document was added to the blockchain is recorded, not when the document was submitted; and the precise time of digital asset creation can be important in IP registration services. Most problematically, timestamping does not prove ownership. However, blockchain attestation services as currently envisioned are an important first step and could be incorporated in 3.0 versions that include other elements in the blockchain ecosystem. Some ideas propose including digital identity to prove ownership and a non-blockchain-based timestamping element for "time document created." A potential technical limitation is the contention that the hash might be less secure when you're hashing very large documents (an 8-GB genome file, for example) compared to small documents (a standard IOU contract), but this concern is unwarranted. The scalability to any file size is the beauty of the hash structure, and it is the hash length (typically 64 characters at present) that is the focus for security, and it could be made longer in the future. The usual threats to hash technology—inverse hashes (an inverse function to attempt to back-compute the hashed content) and collisions (two different files produce the same hash)—are limited in the way hashes are currently used in blockchain.

Virtual Notary, Bitnotar, and Chronobit

Virtual Notary (*http://virtual-notary.org/*) is another project that similarly conceptualizes the need and fulfillment of these kinds of blockchain attestation services. Like Proof of Existence, Virtual Notary does not store files but instead provides a certificate that attests to the file's contents at the moment of submission. The service provides a certificate virtual notary-type service for many different "file types" such as documents, web pages, Twitter feeds, stock prices, exchange rates, weather conditions, DNS entries, email address verifications, university affiliations, real estate values, statements and contracts, and random-number drawing. Files can be in any format, including Microsoft Word, PDF, JPG, PNG, TXT, and PPT (Microsoft Power-Point). The site generates a certificate that can be downloaded from the site, and also offers the other side of the service—examining existing certificates. Virtual Notary's aim is to provide a digital, neutral, dispassionate witness for recording online facts and conveying them to third parties in a trustworthy manner, a critical resource as a larger fraction of our lives is now digital.[102] Two other blockchain timestamp projects are Bitnotar (*http://bit.ly/bitnotar*) and Chronobit (*https://github.com/goblin/chrono bit*). A similar blockchain-based project for contract signing is Pavilion.io, which provides the service much cheaper than Adobe EchoSign or DocuSign; contracts are free to send and only one mBTC to sign.[103] Two other virtual notary projects are Blocksign (*https://blocksign.com/*) and btcluck (*http://bit.ly/btcluck*).

Monegraph: Online Graphics Protection

One digital-art protection project built and intended as a proof of concept using the blockchain ledger Bitcoin 3.0 applications related to new methods of proof is Monegraph (*http://www.monegraph.com/*), whose slogan is "because some art belongs in chains." Using this (currently free) application, individuals can facilitate the monetization of their online graphics—digital media they have already created and posted on the Web—by registering their assets. Just as Bitcoin verifies currency ownership, Monegraph verifies property ownership; this is an example of the smart property application of the blockchain. Monegraph could be a complementary service or feature for stock photo image and graphic repository websites like Shutterstock or Getty Images, possibly adding future functionality related to image use enforcement and tracking.

Monegraph works in a two-step process using Twitter, Namecoin, and Monegraph. Namecoin is used because it is an altcoin that can be used to verify DNS registrations in an automated, decentralized way; any similar DNS confirmation service could be used.[104] First, to stake the claim, the user goes to *http://www.monegraph.com/*, gives it permission to sign in to her Twitter account (via the standardized Twitter API OAuth token), and supplies the URL of the graphic, upon which Monegraph automatically tweets a link to that image in the correct format. Second, to record the title, after Monegraph tweets the link to the image, it provides a block of code for the user to copy and paste into the Namecoin client. The user initiates a new transaction in the Namecoin wallet and adds the block of code as the key and value in the Namecoin transaction (you can see the transaction here: *http://bit.ly/monegraph_verification*). Only one copy of a digital image can ever have a valid Monegraph signature. Monegraph images are just ordinary image files, so they can be duplicated and distributed like any other images, but only the original file will pass validation against the Monegraph system.

A related digital art and copyright protection project is Ascribe (*https://www.ascribe.io/*), which is aimed at providing an underlying infrastructure for IP registry. The company is building what it calls an "ownership layer" for digital property in the form of a service to register and transfer copyright. Although existing copyright law offers creators protection against infringement and the right to commercialize, there is no simple, global interface to register, license, and transfer copyright. The Ascribe service aims to address this, registering a digital work with the service hashes and timestamping it onto the blockchain. An earlier step in the registration process uses machine learning to detect and resolve any prior-art challenges. Ownership rights can then be transferred, which enables secondary markets for digital IP. The service handles digital fine art, photos, logos, music, books, blog posts, tweets, 3D CAD files, and more. Users need no prior knowledge of the intricacies of the blockchain, copyright law, or machine learning to benefit from the service. The bulk of Ascribe's users are marketplaces and white-label web services that use Ascribe in the background, though individual users can use the site directly, as well.

Digital Asset Proof as an Automated Feature

In the future, digital asset protection in the form of blockchain registry could be an automatically applied standardized feature of digital asset publication. For certain classes of assets or websites, digital asset protection could be invoked at the moment of publication of any digital content. Some examples could include GitHub commits, blog posts, tweets, Instagram/Twitpic photos, and forum participations. Digital asset protection could be offered just as travel insurance is with airline ticket purchases. At account setup with Twitter, blogging sites, wikis, forums, and GitHub, the user could approve micropayments for digital asset registration (by supplying a Bitcoin wallet address). Cryptocurrency now as the embedded economic layer of the Web provides microcontent with functionality for micropayment and microIPprotection. Cryptocurrency provides the structure for this, whether microcontent is tokenized and batched into blockchain transactions or digital assets are registered themselves with their own blockchain addresses. Blockchain attestation services could also be deployed more extensively not just for IP registry, but more robustly to meet other related needs in the publishing industry, such as rights transfer and content licensing.

Batched Notary Chains as a Class of Blockchain Infrastructure

It is important to remember that this is only the outset of what could blossom into a full-fledged blockchain economy with blockchain technology enabling every aspect of human endeavor, the blockchain being like the Internet, and the blockchain as the fifth wave of the Internet. In this vein, it is possible that all current blockchain-related activity could be seen as early-stage prototypes looking back from some future moment. What are piecemeal services now could be collected into classes of blockchain services.

From the point of view of overall design principles for the blockchain infrastructure, we would expect to see these classes of sector-specific functionality arriving. Not just separate blockchain notary services, but a new class of notary chains themselves as part of the evolving blockchain infrastructure. Notary chains are an example of a DAO/DAC, a more complicated group of operations that together perform a class of functions incorporating blockchain technology. In this case, this is the idea of notary chains as a class of blockchain protocols for attestation services. For example, it might be more efficient to post batches of transactions as opposed to every individual transaction (requiring the greater-than-zero mining cost). Notary blocks could be composed of the hashes of many digitally notarized assets; the blocks themselves could then be hashed so that the notary block is the unit that is inscribed into the blockchain, making more efficient use of the system rather than every single digital artifact that has been notarized. Because hashes are a one-way function, the existence of the block-level hash in the Bitcoin blockchain constitutes proof of the existence of the subhashes.[105] Moving blockchain design into such an "industrial" DAO/DAC phase brings up interesting questions about how the optimal mix of hierarchical and decentralized architectures will play out in large-scale design architectures. Factom (*http://www.factom.org/*) is a project developing the idea of batched transaction upload in blocks to the blockchain, using the blockchain attestation/notary hash functionality to batch transactions as a means of avoiding blockchain bloat.

Personal Thinking Blockchains

More speculatively for the farther future, the notion of blockchain technology as the automated accounting ledger, the quantized-level tracking device, could be extensible to yet another category of record keeping and administration. There could be "personal thinking chains" as a life-logging storage and backup mechanism. The concept is "blockchain technology + *in vivo* personal connectome" to encode and make useful in a standardized compressed data format all of a person's thinking. The data could be captured via intracortical recordings, consumer EEGs, brain/computer interfaces, cognitive nanorobots, and other methodologies. Thus, thinking could be instantiated in a blockchain—and really all of an individual's subjective experience, possibly eventually consciousness, especially if it's more precisely defined. After they're on the blockchain, the various components could be administered and transacted—for example, in the case of a post-stroke memory restoration.

Just as there has not been a good model with the appropriate privacy and reward systems that the blockchain offers for the public sharing of health data and quantified-self-tracking data, likewise there has not been a model or means of sharing mental performance data. In the case of mental performance data, there is even more stigma attached to sharing personal data, but these kinds of "life-streaming + blockchain technology" models could facilitate a number of ways to share data privately, safely, and remuneratively. As mentioned, in the vein of life logging, there could be personal thinking blockchains to capture and safely encode all of an individual's mental performance, emotions, and subjective experiences onto the blockchain, at minimum for backup and to pass on to one's heirs as a historical record. Personal mindfile blockchains could be like a next generation of Fitbit or Apple's iHealth on the iPhone 6, which now automatically captures 200+ health metrics and sends them to the cloud for data aggregation and imputation into actionable recommendations. Similarly, personal thinking blockchains could be easily and securely recorded (assuming all of the usual privacy concerns with blockchain technology are addressed) and mental performance recommendations made to individuals through services such as Siri or Amazon's Alexa voice assistant, perhaps piped seamlessly through personal brain/computer interfaces and delivered as both conscious and unconscious suggestions.

Again perhaps speculatively verging on science fiction, ultimately the whole of a society's history might include not just a public records and document repository, and an Internet archive of all digital activity, but also the *mindfiles* of individuals. Mindfiles could include the recording of every "transaction" in the sense of capturing every thought and emotion of every entity, human and machine, encoding and archiving this activity into life-logging blockchains.

Blockchain Government

Another important application developing as part of Blockchain 3.0 is blockchain government; that is, the idea of using blockchain technology to provide services traditionally provided by nation-states in a decentralized, cheaper, more efficient, personalized manner. Many new and different kinds of governance models and services might be possible using blockchain technology. Blockchain governance takes advantage of the public record-keeping features of blockchain technology: the blockchain as a universal, permanent, continuous, consensus-driven, publicly auditable, redundant, record-keeping repository. The blockchain could become both the mechanism for governing in the present, and the repository of all of a society's documents, records, and history for use in the future—a society's universal record-keeping system. Not all of the concepts and governance services proposed here necessarily need blockchain technology to function, but there might be other benefits to implementing them with blockchain technology, such as rendering them more trustworthy, and in any case, part of a public record.

One implication of blockchain governance is that government could shift from being the forced one-size-fits-all "greater good" model at present to one that can be tailored to the needs of individuals. Imagine a world of governance services as individualized as Starbucks coffee orders. An example of personalized governance services might be that one resident pays for a higher-tier waste removal service that includes composting, whereas a neighbor pays for a better school package. Personalization in government services, instead of the current one-size-fits-all paradigm, could be orchestrated and delivered via the blockchain. One example of more granular government services could be a situation in which smart cities issue Roadcoin to compensate passing-by drivers for lost #QualityofLife in road construction projects. Likewise, there could be Accidentcoin that those involved in an accident pay to similarly compensate passing-by drivers for lost #QualityofLife; payment could be immediate, and shifted later as insurance companies assess blame.

In science-fiction parlance, it could be said that *franchulates* as envisioned in Neal Stephenson's *Snow Crash* are finally on the horizon.[106] Franchulates are the concept of

---

a combination of a franchise and consulate, businesses that provide fee-based quasigovernmental services consumed by individuals as any other product or service, a concept that blockchain governance could make possible. One attractive aspect of the franchulates concept is the attitudinal shift: the idea that governments need to become more like businesses and less of a default monopoly provider of government services; they should have a more proactive relationship with consumer-citizens, offering value propositions and services that are demanded and valued by different market segments of constituents.

Another implication of blockchain governance is that one vision behind "government on the blockchain" or "putting a nation on the blockchain" is that a more truly representative democracy might be obtained. One way of effectuating this is, rather than having to rely on human agents as representatives, using blockchain smart contracts and DACs. Having many fewer people involved in the governance apparatus could potentially mean smaller, less costly government, less partisanship, and less special-interest lobbyist-directed government. As blockchain technology makes financial systems more efficient, squeezing the marginal cost down to zero, so too could blockchain technology reconfigure the tasks of governance and public administration. The costs savings of smaller government could proceed directly to Guaranteed Basic Income initiatives, promoting equality and political participation in society and easing the transition to the automation economy.

The advent of the blockchain and decentralized models calls into question more generally the ongoing validity of population-sized pooled models like government and insurance that have been de facto standards because other models were not yet possible. However, pooled models might no longer make economic or political sense. Consensus-driven models could be a superior solution economically and offer a more representative and equitable way of interacting with reality, moving to an open frame of eradicating situations of illiberty.[107] The blockchain-as-an-information-technology idea is further underscored in blockchain governance as a new, more efficient system for organizing, administering, coordinating, and recording all human interactions, whether business, government, or personal. The advent of blockchain technology calls into question the more effective execution of government services, but also government-backed rights, which in some cases by design do not (and should not) respect individuality. So far, most projects have addressed only the governance services side, so there is an opportunity to develop interesting blockchain-based models for rights enforcement.

Decentralized Governance Services

Choose your government and choose your services. This is the idea of putting the nation-state on the blockchain, in the sense of offering borderless, decentralized, opt-in blockchain-based governance services.[108] These kinds of services could include an ID system based on reputation, dispute resolution, voting, national income distribution, and registration of all manner of legal documents such as land deeds, wills, childcare contracts, marriage contracts, and corporate incorporations. In fact, the blockchain—with its structure that accommodates secure identities, multiple contracts, and asset management—makes it ideal for situations such as marriage because it means a couple can tie their wedding contract to a shared savings account (e.g., a Bitcoin wallet) and to a childcare contract, land deed, and any other relevant documents for a secure future together.[109]

Indeed, the world's first blockchain-recorded marriage occurred at Disneyworld, Florida, on October 5, 2014 (Figure 3-2). The marriage was submitted to the Bitcoin blockchain, using the blockchain's property of being an online public registry. The vows were transmitted in the text annotation field, embedded in a Bitcoin transaction of 0.1 Bitcoins ($32.50), to appear permanently in the blockchain ledger.[110] Liberty.me CEO Jeffrey Tucker officiated at the ceremony and discussed the further benefits of denationalized marriage in the context of marriage equality, how marriage can be more equitably and permissively recorded and recognized in a blockchain than in many states and nations at present.[111] One indication that the "blockchain as public documents registry" has truly arrived would be, for example, if there were to be corresponding Bitcoin prediction markets contracts for events in the couple's life, such as having children, purchasing real estate, and even potentially filing for divorce (which would also be logged on the blockchain), and the inevitable social science research to follow showing that blockchain marriages last longer (or not) than their religious or civil counterparts.

Figure 3-2. World's first Bitcoin wedding, David Mondrus and Joyce Bayo, Disneyworld, Florida, October 5, 2014 (image credit: Bitcoin Magazine, Ruben Alexander)

Blockchain-based governance systems could offer a range of services traditionally provided by governments, all of which could be completely voluntary, with user-citizens opting in and out at will. Just as Bitcoin is emerging as a better alternative to fiat currency in some situations (cheaper, more efficient, easier to transmit, immediately received, and a superior payments mechanism), the same could be true for blockchain-based governance services. The same services a traditional "fiat" government carries out could be delivered in a cheaper, distributed, voluntary way by using blockchain technology. The blockchain lends itself well to being a universal, permanent, searchable, irrevocable public records repository. All government legal documents such as deeds, contracts, and identification cards can be stored on the blockchain. Identity systems such as blockchain-based passports would need to achieve critical mass adoption in order to be recognized, just as Bitcoin does in the case of being recognized and being widely usable as money. One project that provides the code for a blockchain-based passport system is the World Citizen project (*https:// github.com/MrChrisJ/World-Citizenship*).[112] The project aims to create world citizenship through affordable decentralized passport services by using available cryptographic tools (Figure 3-3).

Figure 3-3. The World Citizen Project's Blockchain-based passport (image credit: Chris Ellis)

A key point is that anyone worldwide can use decentralized government services; just because you live in a particular geography should not restrict you to certain government services and mean that you have only one government provider. Governments have been a monopoly, but with blockchain government services in the global Internet-connected world, this need not be the case any longer. The possibility of global currencies like Bitcoin and global government services bring up important questions about the shifting nature of nation-states and what their role should be in the future. A country might be something like a hometown, where you are from, but not in sharp relief in day-to-day activities in a world where currency, finance, professional activities, collaboration, government services, and record keeping are on the blockchain. Further, Bitcoin provides a transition to a world in which individuals are increasingly mobile between nation-states and could benefit from one overall governance system rather than the host of inefficiencies in complying with multiple nation-states. As is standard with cryptocurrency code, decentralized governance software, too, would be open source and forkable, so that anyone can create his own blockchain nation and government services in this collaborative platform for DIYgovernance.

In the area of titling and deeds, as Bitcoin is to remittances, decentralized blockchain government services is to the implementation of a property ownership registry, and could be the execution of the detailed plans set forth by development economists such as Hernando de Soto.[113] Decentralized blockchain-based government services such as public documents registries and titling could be a useful tool for scaling the efforts already in place by organizations such as de Soto's Institute for Liberty and Democracy, or ILD (http://www.ild.org.pe), which has programs to document, evaluate, and diagnose the extralegal sector and bring it into alignment with the legal system. A universal blockchain-based property registry could bring much-needed ownership documentation, transferability, transactability, value capture, and opportunity and mobilization to emerging markets where these structures do not exist or are nascent (and simultaneously, potential business for its blockchain service cousin, dispute resolution). As some countries in Africa were able to leapfrog directly to cellular telephone networks without installing copper wire infrastructure (and some countries might be able to leapfrog directly to preventive medicine with personalized genomics[114]), so too could emerging-market countries leapfrog directly to the implementation of blockchain property registries. Other blockchain government services could facilitate similar leapfrogging—for example, speeding Aadhar's (the world's largest biometric database[115]) efforts in issuing national ID cards to the 25 percent of Indians who did not have them, and helping to eliminate inefficiencies in national ID card programs due to issues like ghost IDs and duplicate IDs.

PrecedentCoin: Blockchain Dispute Resolution

Another Blockchain 3.0 project focuses exclusively on using the blockchain for more effective dispute resolution. Precedent (http://precedent.io/) is conceptually like "The People's Court or Judge Judy on the blockchain." So far there has been no way to take advantage of a centralized repository of precedents used to resolve disputes, so Precedent is developing a concept, framework, altcoin, and community to implement a decentralized autonomous legal procedure organization (as described in further detail in "The Precedent Protocol Whitepaper." (https://github.com/mdelias/precedent) Precedent's "polycentric decentralized legal system" makes it possible for individual users to pick the legal system and features they like, emphasizing the ongoing theme of blockchain-enabled personalization of governance and legal systems. The Precedent legal/dispute-resolution community is incentivized to develop with the community coin, PrecedentCoin or nomos.

In the same way that a decentralized community of miners maintains the Bitcoin blockchain by checking, confirming, and recording new transactions, so too functionally do "dispute precedent miners" in the Precedent community by entering new disputes, resolved disputes, and precedents on the dispute resolution blockchain (the blockchain entries are links to securely stored off-chain content with the dispute/precedent details). Precedent runs as a blockchain metaprotocol overlay (structurally like Counterparty). Proof of precedent is envisioned as part of the system's consensus mechanism (analogous to proof of work or proof of stake in Bitcoin mining). The Precedent system is radically peer-to-peer; users dictate what it means for a dispute to be justiciable (appropriate or suitable for adjudication), and they can fork the protocol if new standards are deemed preferable. The tokenized altcoin, Precedentcoin or nomos, is used for community economic functions like paying to submit a dispute to the network and remunerating "miners" for community dispute resolution tasks (conceptually like community "jurors" or "citizen dispute resolvers").

It should be noted that, as the project points out in a white paper, "The Precedent Protocol is strictly concerned with the justiciability of the dispute in question and is wholly agnostic to the justness or fairness of the outcome." Thus, there is potential risk for abuse, in the form of buying or collectively achieving a strange or unfair decision by consensus. The project aims to decide only the justiciability of a dispute—the point of law, not the point of fact.

Liquid Democracy and Random-Sample Elections

Other blockchain governance efforts focus more directly on developing systems to make democracy more effective. In the model of a DAS (distributed autonomous society), there could be a need to set forth standardized principles for consensus-based decentralized governance systems, and decentralized voting systems such as that offererd by BitCongress (*http://www.bitcongress.org/*).[116] Other projects focus on other ideas such as delegative democracy, a form of democratic control where voting power is vested in delegates, as opposed to representatives (as many congressional and parliamentary models today). One such project is Liquid Democracy (*http://liquidfeedback.org/*), which provides open source software to facilitate proposition development and decision making.

In the Liquid Democracy system, a party member can assign a proxy vote to any other member, thereby assigning a personal delegate instead of voting for a representative. A member can give her vote to another member for all issues, for a particular policy area, or for only a particular decision for any length of time. That vote can be rescinded at any time. Under this system, a person can become a delegate for multiple members within a polity very quickly, wielding the political power normally reserved for elected representatives as a result. But, a person can lose this power just as quickly. This is the "liquid" in Liquid Democracy, a process that can also be referred to as "transitive delegation." If someone is respected as a trusted expert in a particular area, he can gain members' votes. As a result, every person within a Liquid Democracy platform is a potential politician.[117] There are clearly many potential issues with the Liquid Democracy platform as currently set forth. One concern is stability and continuity over time, which could be resolved with agent reputation mechanisms, broadly confirmable and transferrable if stored in an accessible blockchain.

The idea of delegated decision making, supported and executed in blockchain-based frameworks might have wide applicability beyond the political voting and policy making context. For example, health is another area for which advocacy, advice, and decision making are often delegated and poorly tracked with almost no accountability. Blockchain technology creates an opportunity for the greater accountability and tracking of such delegation. For example, the bioethical nuances of delegated medical decision making articulated in the book *Deciding for Others*, by Allen Buchanan, could be implemented in Liquid Democracy structure.[118] This could improve health care–related decision making, and enable a system of decentralized advocacy, as many individuals do not have adequate informed advisors on hand to act on their behalf. In the farther future, cultural technologies such as the blockchain could become a mechanism for applied ethics.

Liquid Democracy is also a proposition development platform. Any member can propose a new idea. If enough other members support the proposition, it moves on to a discussion phase, at which point it can be modified and alternatives put forward. Of the proposals that are offered, those with enough support are put up for a vote. A vote is made using the Schultz method of preferential voting, which ensures that votes are not split by almost identical "cloned" proposals (like double-spend problem for votes). All of this is coordinated in the online platform. The voting system can run at different levels of transparency: disclosed identity, anonymity, or a hybrid system of authenticated pseudonymity. An unresolved issue is how binding decisions made by the Liquid Democracy system might be and what enforcement or follow-up mechanisms can be included in the software. Perhaps initially Liquid Democracy could serve as an intermediary tool for coordinating votes and indicating directional outcomes.

Ideas for a more granular application of democracy have been proposed for years, but it is only now with the Internet and the advent of systems like blockchain technology that these kinds of complex and dynamic decision-making mechanisms become feasible to implement in real-world contexts. For example, the idea for delegative democracy in the form of transitive voting was initially proposed by Lewis Carroll (the author of *Alice in Wonderland*) in his book *The Principles of Parliamentary Representation*.[119]

Random-Sample Elections

In addition to delegative democracy, another idea that could be implemented with blockchain governance is random-sample elections. In random-sample elections, randomly selected voters receive a ballot in the mail and are directed to an election website that features candidate debates and activist statements. As articulated by cryptographer David Chaum,[120] the idea is that (like the ideal of a poll) randomly sampled voters would be more representative (or could at least include underrepresented voters) and give voters more time to deliberate on issues privately at home, seeking their own decision-making resources rather than being swayed by advertising.[121] Blockchain technology could be a means of implementing random-sample elections in a large-scale, trustable, pseudonymous way.

Futarchy: Two-Step Democracy with Voting + Prediction Markets

Another concept is *futarchy*, a two-level process by which individuals first vote on generally specified outcomes (like "increase GDP"), and second, vote on specific proposals for achieving these outcomes. The first step would be carried out by regular voting processes, the second step via prediction markets. Prediction market voting could be by different cryptocurrencies (the EconomicVotingCoin or EnvironmentalPolicyVotingCoin) or other economically significant tokens. Prediction market voting is investing/speculating, taking a bet on one or the other side of a proposal, betting on the proposal that you want to win. For example, you might buy the "invest in new biotechnologies contract" as what you think is the best means of achieving the "increase in GDP" objective, as opposed to other contracts like the "invest in automated agriculture contract"). As with random-sampling elections, blockchain technology could more efficiently implement the futarchy concept in an extremely large-scale manner (decentralized, trusted, recorded, pseudonymous). The futarchy concept is described in shorthand as "vote for values, bet on beliefs," an idea initially proposed by economist Robin Hanson,[122] and expounded in the blockchain context by Ethereum project founder Vitalik Buterin.[123] This is a quintessential example of the potential transformative power of blockchain technology. There is the possibility that voting and preference-specification models (like futarchy's two-tiered voting structure using blockchain technology) could became a common, widespread norm and feature or mechanism for all complex multiparty human decision making. One effect of this could be a completely new level of coordinated human activity that is orders of magnitude more complex than at present. Of course, any new governance structure including futarchy has ample room for abuse, and mechanisms for restricting coercion and outright results hacking are incorporated to some degree but would need to be improved upon in more robust models.

For the agreed-upon consensus necessary to register blockchain transactions, there could be at least two models, and potentially many more in the future. The first consensus mechanism is the mining operation: with the aid of software, miners review, confirm, and register transactions. The second consensus mechanism is prediction markets. An event might be assumed to be true if enough independent unaffiliated persons have voted their opinion that it is true in a prediction market. Truthcoin (*http://www.truthcoin.info/*) is such a blockchain-based, trustless, peer-to-peer prediction marketplace that hopes to resolve some problems with traditional prediction markets, such as bias in voters, and integrate the prediction market concept with the remunerative coin and public records structure of Bitcoin.[124] Even farther, Truthcoin aims to provide a trustless oracle service, registering what might be relevant events of record in the blockchain. Some examples of "information items" of interest would be the current interest rate, the daily high temperature, and cryptocurrency daily high and low prices and trading volume. For blockchain-based smart contract operations, independent oracles providing information are a key component in the value chain. For example, blockchain-based mortgage might have certain interest rate reset dates in the future that could be automatically implemented upon having a trustable source of future information, such as that registered in a blockchain by a reputable independent oracle, like Truthcoin.

Societal Maturity Impact of Blockchain Governance

A side benefit of blockchain governance is that it might force individuals and societies to grow into a new level of maturity in how topics like governance, authority, independence, and participation are conceptualized and executed. We are not used to governance being a personal responsibility and a peer-to-peer system as opposed to something externally imposed by a distant centralized institution. We are not used to many aspects of blockchain technology, like having to back up our money, but we learn appropriate savviness and new behaviors and conceptualizations when adopting new technologies. We are not used to decentralized political authority and autonomy.

However, we have matured into the reception of decentralized authority in other contexts. Authority floating freely has already happened in other industries such as information, wherein the news and publishing industry became decentralized with blogging and the restructuring of the media industry. Entertainment is similar, with corporate media properties existing alongside YouTube channels, and individuals uploading their own content to the Web. The value chain has exploded into the long-tail format, and individuals became their own taste makers and quality arbiters. A crucial twenty-first-century skill is that individuals must examine content and think for themselves about its quality and validity. The Bitcoin revolution is the same thing happening now with currency, economics, finance, and monetary policy. It might seem harder to let go of centralized authority in matters of government and economics as opposed to culture and information, but there is no reason that social maturity could not develop similarly in this context.

CHAPTER 4

Blockchain 3.0: Efficiency and Coordination Applications Beyond Currency, Economics, and Markets

Blockchain Science: Gridcoin, Foldingcoin

As blockchain technology could revolutionize the operation of other fields, innovators are starting to envision how the concepts might apply to science. So far, the main thread is related to peer-to-peer distributed computing projects for which individual volunteers provide unused computing cycles to Internet-based distributed computing projects. Two notable projects are SETI@home (the Search for Extraterrestrial Intelligence, which uses contributed computing cycles to help analyze radio signals from space, searching for signs of extraterrestrial intelligence), and Folding@home (a Stanford University project for which computing cycles are used to simulate protein folding, for computational drug design and other molecular dynamics problems). Per blockchain technology, remunerative coin has been set up to reward participants in both the SETI@home and Folding@home projects. For SETI@home, there is Gridcoin (*http://www.gridcoin.us/*), which is the remunerative coin available to all BOINC (Berkeley Open Infrastructure for Network Computing) projects, the infrastructure upon which SETI@home runs. For Folding@home, there is FoldingCoin (*http://foldingcoin.net/*), a Counterparty token that runs and is exchangeable to the more liquid XCP cryptocurrency (and therefore out to Bitcoin and fiat currency) via the Counterparty wallet (Counterwallet).

A more fundamental use of the blockchain for science could be addressing the wastefulness of the mining network, which consumes massive amounts of electricity. Instead of being used to crunch arbitrary numbers, perhaps the extensive processing power could be applied to the more practical task of solving existing science problems. However, a mining algorithm must meet very specific conditions, like generating code strings or hashes that are easily verifiable in one direction but not in reverse, which is not the structure of traditional scientific computing problems.[125] There are some cryptocurrency projects trying to make blockchain mining scientifically useful—for example, Primecoin (*http://primecoin.io/*), for which miners are required to find long chains of prime numbers (Cunningham chains and bi-twin chains) instead of SHA256 hashes (the random guesses of a specific number issued by mining software programs based on given general parameters).[126] There is an opportunity for greater progress in this area to reformulate supercomputing and desktop grid computing problems, which have been organized mainly in a massively parallel fashion, into a mining-compatible format to take advantage of otherwise wasted computing cycles.[127]

Gridcoin, if not solving the problem of using otherwise wasted mining cycles, at least tries to align incentives by encouraging miners to also contribute computing cycles: miners are compensated at a much higher rate (5 GRC versus a maximum of 150 GRC) for mining a currency block when also contributing computing cycles. A typical complaint about blockchain technology is the wastefulness of mining, both in terms of unused computing cycles and electricity consumption. The media presents estimates of power consumption such as "the Eiffel Tower could stay lit for 260 years with the energy used to mine Bitcoins since 2009,"[128] and that in 2013 Bitcoin mining was consuming about 982 megawatt hours a day (enough to power 31,000 homes in the United States, or half a Large Hadron Collider),[129] at a cost of $15 million a day.[130] However, the comparison metric is unclear; should these figures be regarded as a little or a lot (and what are the direct economic benefits of the Eiffel Tower and the LHC, for that matter)? Bitcoin proponents counter that the blockchain model is vastly cheaper when you consider the fully loaded cost of the current financial system, which includes the entire infrastructure of physical plant bank branch offices and personnel. They point out that the cost to deliver $100 via the blockchain is much cheaper than traditional methods. Still, there is concern over how Bitcoin could eliminate its wasteful consumption of electricity for mining while continuing to maintain the blockchain, and 3.0 innovations could be expected. One response is cryptocurrencies that are apparently more energy efficient, such as Mintcoin (*http://mintcoin.cc/*).

Community Supercomputing

SETI@home and Folding@home are community supercomputing projects in the sense that a community of individual volunteers contributes the raw resource of computing cycles; they are not involved in setting the research agenda. A more empowered model of community supercomputing would be using the resource-allocation mechanism of the blockchain to allow noninstitutional researchers access to supercomputing time for their own projects of interest. In a model like Kickstarter, individuals could list projects requiring supercomputing time and find other project collaborators and funders, soliciting and rewarding activities with appcoin or site-coin. An early project in this area, Zennet, has been announced which may allow community users to specify their own supercomputing projects and access shared desktop grid resources via a blockchain structure. Citizen science data analysis projects are under way and were perhaps initially demonstrated in the example of mass collaboration on open data sets in the book *Wikinomics* (2008).[131] The difference is in liberty extending: now using the blockchain means that these kinds of citizen science projects can be deployed at much larger scale—in fact, the largest scale—at a tier at which (per resource constraints) citizen scientists do not currently have access. *Wikinomics* and other examples have documented the scientifically valid contributions of citizen science as a channel.[132] Projects such as DIYweathermodeling, for example, could have the benefit of getting citizen scientists involved in contributing evidence to large-scale issues like the climate change debate.

Global Public Health: Bitcoin for Contagious Disease Relief

Another application of blockchain health is in global public health, for the efficient, immediate, targeted delivery of aid funds for supplies in the case of crises like Ebola and other contagious disease breakouts.[133] Traditional banking flows hamper the immediacy of aid delivery in crisis situations, as opposed to Bitcoin, which can be delivered immediately to specific publicly auditable trackable addresses. Individual peer-to-peer aid as well as institutional aid could be contributed via Bitcoin. In emerging markets (often with cellphone penetration or 70 percent or higher) there are a number of SMS Bitcoin wallets and delivery mechanisms, such as 37Coins (*https://www.37coins.com/*)[134] and Coinapult (*https://coinapult.com/*), and projects such as Kipochi (*https://www.kipochi.com/*)[135] that are integrated with commonly used mobile finance platforms like M-Pesa (in Kenya, for example, 31 percent of the GDP is spent through mobile phones[136]). Apps could be built on infectious disease tracking sites like Healthmap (*http://healthmap.org/*) and FluTrackers (*http://www.flutrackers.com/*) to include Bitcoin donation functionality or remunerative appcoin more generally.

Charity Donations and the Blockchain—Sean's Outpost

Perhaps the world's best-known Bitcoin-accepting charity is Sean's Outpost (*http://seansoutpost.com/donate/*), a homeless outreach nonprofit organization based in Pensacola, Florida. Capitalizing on the trend of individuals receiving Bitcoin and not having any local venues to spend it in or otherwise not knowing what to do with it, and Bitcoin startups needing to demo how Bitcoin is sent on the Web, Sean's Outpost has been able to raise significant donor contributions and undertake projects like a nine-acre "Satoshi Forest" sanctuary for the homeless.[137]

Blockchain Genomics

The democratization and freedom-enhancing characteristics of the blockchain seen in many projects also apply in the case of *consumer genomics*, which is the concept of uplifting organizations to the blockchain (to the cloud in a decentralized, secure way) to escape the limitations of local jurisdictional laws and regulation. That there is a need for this does not necessarily signal illegal "bad players" with malicious intent; rather, it indicates a lack of trust, support, relevance, and espousal of shared values in local jurisdictional governments. Traditional government 1.0 is becoming outdated as a governance model in the blockchain era, especially as we begin to see the possibility to move from paternalistic, one-size-fits-all structures to a more granular personalized form of government. Genomics can be added to the list of examples of uplifting transnational organizations to the decentralized blockchain cloud like ICANN, WikiLeaks, Twitter, Wikipedia, GitHub, and new business registrations as DACs. Transnational blockchain genomics makes sense in the context of the right to personal information (the right to one's own genetic information) being seen as a basic human right, especially given the increasing cost feasibility per plummeting genomic sequencing costs.

In one view, consumer genomics can be seen as a classic case of personal freedom infringement. In many European countries and the United States, paternalistic government policy (influenced by the centralized strength of the medical-industry lobby) prevents individuals from having access to their own genetic data. Even in countries where personal genomic information is used in health care, there is most often no mechanism for individuals to get access to their own underlying data. In the United States, prominent genomic researchers have tried to make a public case that the "FDA [Food and Drug Administration] is overcautious on consumer genomics,"[138] and established in studies that there is no detrimental effect to individuals having access to their own genomic data.[139] In fact, the opposite might be true: in the humans-as-rational-agents model, 80 percent of individuals learning of a potential genetic predisposition for Alzheimer's disease modified their life-style behaviors (e.g., exercise and vitamin consumption) as a result.[140] Other news accounts continue to chronicle how individuals are seeking their own genomic data and finding it useful—for example, to learn about Alzheimer's and heart disease risk.[141]

As a result of paternalistic purview, and no clear government policies for the preventive medicine era, US-based consumer genomics services have closed (deCODEme[142]), directed their services exclusively toward a physician-permissioning model (Pathway Genomics, Navigenics), or been forced to greatly curtail their consumer-targeted services (23andMe[143]). In response, blockchain-based genomic services could be an idea for providing low-cost genomic sequencing to individuals, making the data available via private key.

One of the largest current transformational challenges in public health and medicine is moving from the current narrowband model of "having only been able to treat diagnosed pathologies" to a completely new data-rich era of preventive medicine for which the goal is maintaining, prolonging, and enhancing baseline health.[144] Such a wellness era is now beginning to be possible through the use of personalized big data as predictive information about potential future conditions. Personalized genomics is a core health data stream for preventive medicine as well as individuals as knowledgeable, self-interested, action-taking agents.[145]

In fact, as of November 2014, a blockchain genomics project, Genecoin (*http://gene coin.me/*), has launched an exploratory website to assess potential consumer interest, positioning the service as a means of backing up your DNA.[146]

Blockchain Genomics 2.0: Industrialized All-Human-Scale Sequencing Solution

At one level, there could be blockchain-enabled services where genomic data is sequenced and made available to individuals by private key outside the jurisdiction of local governments. However, at another higher level, as a practical matter, to achieve the high-throughput sequencing needed for all seven billion humans, larger-scale models are required, and blockchain technology could be a helpful mechanism for the realization of this project. Individuals ordering their genomes piecemeal through consumer genomic services is an initial proof of concept in some ways (and a health literacy tool as well as a possible delivery mechanism for personal results and recommendations), but not an "all-human-scale" solution for sequencing. Blockchain technology, in the form of a universal model for record keeping and data storage and access (a secure, decentralized, pseudonymous file structure for data stored and accessed in the cloud) could be the technology that is needed to move into the next phase of industrialized genomic sequencing. This applies to genomic sequencing generally as an endeavor, irrespective of the personal data rights access issue. Sequencing all humans is just one dimension of sequencing demand; there is also the sequencing of all plants, animals, crops, viruses, bacteria, disease-strain pathogens, microbiomes, cancer genomes, proteomes, and so on, to name a few use cases.

There is a scale production and efficiency argument for blockchain-based transnational genomic services. To move to large-scale sequencing as a "universal human society," the scope and scale of sequencing and corresponding information processing workloads suggests not just transnationality, but more important, heavy integration with the cloud (genomic data is too big for current forms of local storage and manipulation), and the blockchain delivers both transnationality and the cloud. Transnational regional centers for genomic sequencing and processing and information management of the sequenced files could be the best way to structure the industry given the cost, expertise, equipment, and scale required. This could be a more efficient solution rather than each country developing its own capabilities. Blockchain technology might be used to achieve a high-throughput level of industrialized genomic sequencing—on the order of millions and billions of genomes, well beyond today's hundreds. In reality, blockchain technology might supply just one aspect of what might be needed; other issues are more critical in achieving industrialized genomic sequencing operations (information processing and data storage is seen as the real bottleneck). However, the blockchain ecosystem is inventing many new methods for other operational areas along the way and might be able to innovate in a complementary manner for a full solution to industrial-scale genomic sequencing, including recasting the problem in different ways as with decentralization concepts.

Blockchain Technology as a Universal Order-of-Magnitude Progress Model

Blockchain technology might be indicative of the kinds of mechanisms and models needed to achieve the next orders-of-magnitude progress in areas like big data, moving to what would currently be conceived as "truly-big-data," and well beyond. Genomic sequencing could be one of the first demonstration contexts of these higher-orders-of-magnitude models for progress.

Genomecoin, GenomicResearchcoin

Even without considering the longer-term speculative possibilities of the complete invention of an industrial-scale all-human genome sequencing project with the blockchain, just adding blockchain technology as a feature to existing sequencing activities could be enabling. Conceptually, this would be like adding coin functionality or blockchain functionality to services like DNAnexus (*https:// www.dnanexus.com/*), a whole-human genome cloud-based storage service. Operating in collaboration with university collaborators (Baylor College of Medicine's Human Genome Sequencing Center) and Amazon Web Services, the DNAnexus solution is perhaps the largest current data store of genomes, having 3,751 whole human genomes and 10,771 exomes (440 terabytes) as of 2013.[147] The progress to date is producing a repository of 4,000 human genomes, out of the possible field of 7 billion humans, which highlights the need for large-scale models in these kinds of big data projects (human whole-genome sequencing). The DNAnexus database is not a public good with open access; only 300 worldwide preapproved genomic researchers have permission to use it. The Genomic Data Commons[148] is a US-government-funded large-scale data warehouse and computational computing project being assembled to focus on genomic research and personalized medicine. In this case, the resource is said to be available to any US-based researcher. This is a good step forward in organizing data into standard unified repositories and allowing access to a certain population. A further step could be using an appcoin like Genomecoin to expand access on a grander scale as a public good fully accessible by any individual worldwide. Further, the appcoin could be the tracking, coordination, crediting, and renumerative mechanism sponsoring collaboration in the Genome Data Commons community. Like the aforementioned *Wikinomics* example, the highest potential possibility for discovery could be in making datasets truly open for diverse sets of individuals and teams from a variety of fields and backgrounds to apply any kind of model they might have developed.

One benefit of "Bitcoin/blockchain-as-economics" is that the technology automatically enables embedded economics as a feature in any system. In the genomic sequencing and storage context, the economics feature could be used in numerous ways, such as obtaining more accurate costs of research (blockchain economics as tracking and accounting) and to remunerate data contributors (whether institutional or individual) with Genomecoin or GenomicResearchcoin (blockchain economics as micropayment remuneration). The economic/accounting tracking features of the blockchain further allows now other foreseen capabilities of the blockchain, such as attribution as an enabler for large-scale human projects (like attribution at the GitHub line item of committed code or digital asset IP-protected ideas). Attribution is a crucial feature for encouraging individual participation in large-scale projects.

Blockchain Health

In the future, there might be different kinds of blockchains (ledgers) for recording and tracking different kinds of processes, and exchanging and providing access to different kinds of assets, including digital health assets. Blockchain health is the idea of using blockchain technology for health-related applications.[149] The key benefit behind blockchain health is that the blockchain provides a structure for storing health data on the blockchain such that it can be analyzed but remain private, with an embedded economic layer to compensate data contribution and use.[150]

Healthcoin

Healthcoin could more broadly be the coin or token for health spending, forcing price discovery and rationalization across health services. Services in national health plans could be denominated and paid in Healthcoin. This could help to improve economic inefficiencies rife within the health-services industry. Price transparency—and a universal price list—could result, such that every time a certain health service is performed, it costs 5 Healthcoin, for example, instead of the current system (in the United States) where each consumer might pay a different amount that is a complex calculation of the multipayor system connecting different insurers and plans.

EMRs on the Blockchain: Personal Health Record Storage

Personal health records could be stored and administered via blockchain like a vast electronic electronic medical record (EMR) system. Taking advantage of the pseudonymous (i.e., coded to a digital address, not a name) nature of blockchain technology and its privacy (private key access only), personal health records could be encoded as digital assets and put on the blockchain just like digital currency. Individuals could grant doctors, pharmacies, insurance companies, and other parties access to their health records as needed via their private key. In addition, services for putting EMRs onto the blockchain could promote a universal format, helping to resolve the issue that even though most large health services providers have moved to an EMR system, they are widely divergent and not sharable or interoperable. The blockchain could provide a universal exchangeable format and storage repository for EMRs at a population-wide scale.

Blockchain Health Research Commons

One benefit of creating standardized EMR repositories is exactly that they are repositories: vast standardized databases of health information in a standardized format accessible to researchers. Thus far, nearly all health data stores have been in inaccessible private silos—for example, data from one of the world's largest longitudinal health studies, the Framingham Heart Study. The blockchain could provide a standardized secure mechanism for digitizing health data into health data commons, which could be made privately available to researchers. One example of this is DNA.bits, a startup that encodes patient DNA records to the blockchain, and makes them available to researchers by private key.[151]

However, it is not just that private health data research commons could be established with the blockchain, but also public health data commons. Blockchain technology could provide a model for establishing a cost-effective public-health data commons. Many individuals would like to contribute personal health data—like personal genomic data from 23andMe, quantified-self tracking device data (FitBit), and health and fitness app data (MapMyRun)—to data research commons, in varying levels of openness/privacy, but there has not been a venue for this. This data could be aggregated in a public-health commons (like Wikipedia for health) that is open to anyone, citizen scientists and institutional researchers alike, to perform data analysis. The hypothesis is that integrating big health data streams (genomics, lifestyle, medical history, etc.) and running machine learning and other algorithms over them might yield correlations and data relationships that could be helpful for wellness maintenance and preventive medicine.[152] In general, health research could be conducted more effectively through the aggregation of personal health record data stored on the blockchain (meaning stored off-chain with pointers on-chain). The economic feature of the blockchain could facilitate research, as well. Users might feel more comfortable contributing their personal health data to a public data commons like the blockchain, first because it is private (data is encrypted and pseudonymous), and second for remuneration in the form of Healthcoin or some other sort of digital token.

Blockchain Health Notary

Notary-type proof-of-existence services are a common need in the health industry. Proof of insurance, test results, prescriptions, status, condition, treatment, and physician referrals are just a few examples of health document–related services often required. The "notary function" as a standard blockchain application is equally well deployed in the context of blockchain health. Health documents can be encoded to the blockchain as digital assets, which could then be verified and confirmed in seconds with encryption technology as opposed to hours or days with traditional technology. The private-key functionality of the blockchain could also make certain health services and results delivery, such as STD screening, more efficient and secure.

Doctor Vendor RFP Services and Assurance Contracts

Blockchain health could create more of a two-way market for all health services. Doctors and health practices could bid to supply medical services needed by patient-consumers. Just as Uber drivers bid for driver assignments with customers, doctor practices could bid for hip replacements and other needed health services—for example, in Healthcoin—at minimum bringing some degree of price transparency and improved efficiency to the health sector. This bidding could be automated via tradenets for another level of autonomy, efficiency, and equality.

Virus Bank, Seed Vault Backup

The third step of blockchain health as a standardized repository and a data research commons is backup and archival, not just in the operational sense based on practitioner needs, but as a historical human data record. This is the use case of the blockchain as a public good. Blockchain backup could provide another security layer to the physical-world practices of virus banks, gene banks, and seed vaults. The blockchain could be the digital instantiation of physical-world storage centers like the Svalbard Global Seed Vault (a secure seedbank containing duplicate samples of worldwide plant seeds), and World Health Organization–designated repositories like the CDC for pathogen storage such as the smallpox virus. A clear benefit is that in the case of disease outbreaks, response time can be hastened as worldwide researchers are private key–permissioned into the genetic sequencing files of pathogens of interest.

Blockchain Learning: Bitcoin MOOCs and Smart Contract Literacy

Blockchain-based smart contracts could have myriad uses. One possibility is smart literacy contracts. Bitcoin MOOCs (massive open online courses) and smart literacy contracts encompass the idea of opening up emerging-market smart-contract learning to all individuals worldwide the same way that traditional MOOCs opened up educational courses to all individuals worldwide. Just as Bitcoin is reinventing the remittances market and bringing about financial inclusion, so too the foreign aid market can be reinvented with blockchain-based, peer-to-peer smart contracts. The concept is like Kiva, Grameen microlending, or Heifer International 2.0, which could include peer-to-peer financial aid, but more importantly allows the configuration of peer-to-peer aid that is not currency-based but personal development-based. Blockchain Learning is decentralized learning contracts.

One way to improve literacy in emerging markets (perhaps the key metric for poverty eradication) could be via decentralized smart contracts for literacy written between a donor/sponsor peer and a learning peer. Much in the way that Bitcoin is the decentralized (very low fee charging, no intermediary) means of exchanging currencies between countries, a decentralized contract system could be helpful for setting up learning contracts directly with students/student groups in a similar peer-to-peer manner, conceptually similar to a personalized Khan Academy curriculum program. Learners would receive Bitcoin, Learncoin, or the local token directly into their digital wallets—like 37Coins, Coinapolt, or Kipochi (used as Bitcoin or converted into local fiat currency)—from worldwide peer donors, and use this to fund their education expenses at school or separately on their own. A key part of the value chain is having a reporting mechanism (enabled and automated by Ethereum smart contracts, for example) to attest to learner progress. Rules embedded in learning smart contracts could automatically confirm the completion of learning modules through standardized online tests (including confirming the learner's digital identity, such as with short-handle names for Bitcoin addresses provided with services like OneName, BitID, and Bithandle). Satisfying the learning contract could then automatically trigger the disbursement of subsequent funds for the next learning modules. Blockchain learning contracts can be coordinated completely on a peer-to-peer basis between the learner and the learning sponsor; and really directly with the automated software contract. Again, the idea is like Kiva or Heifer International (i.e., peer-to-peer direct) for blockchain literacy for individualized learning contracts.

Learncoin

Learncoin could be the currency of the smart contract literacy system, with schools, student groups, or individuals issuing their own token: MthelieLearncoin, Huruma Girls High School tokens, or PS 135 tokens (that all convert to Learncoin, and to Bitcoin). School fundraising in any area worldwide could be conducted with Learncoin and LocalSchoolName tokens. Just as physician RFPs make the health services market two-sided, students or student groups could post their open learning contracts (or funding needs and budget) to a Learning Exchange, which could be fulfilled by learning-funders on the other side of the transaction.

Learning Contract Exchanges

Learning contract exchanges could apply in a much broader sense—for example, as a universal learning model. This could apply to government workforce retraining, graduate students, and employees within corporations. Learning contract exchanges could be a way of reinventing or improving the orchestration of the continuing professional education (CPE) programs required for many fields like law, information technology, and medicine. Learning contracts in the development context could be extended to many use cases in emerging markets. There could be many categories of "literacy" contracts, such as basic reading for elementary school children, but also for every area of education, such as vocational learning (technical literacy and agricultural literacy), business literacy, social literacy, and leadership literacy.

Blockchain Academic Publishing: Journalcoin

As every category of organized human activity has moved onto the Internet and currently has the possibility of being reinvented and made more efficient, fair, and otherwise attribute-enabled with the blockchain, so too could academic publishing be put on the blockchain. There have been innovations toward openness in the academic publishing field, such as open-access journals, which although they provide open access to article content instead of keeping it behind a paywall, force authors to support possibly prohibitive publication fees. So far, the Bitcoin convention of making open source code available by publishing software for cryptocurrency blockchains and protocols on GitHub has extended to some forms of "academic" publishing in the area, too, as white papers are posted as "Readme files" on GitHub. For example, there is blockchain venture capitalist David Johnston's Dapp paper ("The General Theory of Decentralized Applications") and Factom's concept for batching the notarization of digital artifacts paper (the "Notary Chains" white paper).

An interesting challenge for academic publishing on the blockchain is not just having an open-access, collaboratively edited, ongoing-discussion-forum journal per existing examples, or open-access, self-published blockchain white papers on GitHub, but to more fundamentally implement the blockchain concepts in blockchain journals. The consideration of what a decentralized direct peer-to-peer model for academic publishing could look like prompts the articulation of the functions that academic publishing provides and how, if these are still required, they might be provided in decentralized models. In terms of "publishing," any manner of making content publicly available on the Web is publishing; one can easily self-publish on blogs, wikis, Twitter, Amazon, and the like. A blockchain model in terms of decentralized peer-to-peer content would be nothing more than a search engine linking one individual's interests with another's published material. This is a decentralized peer-to-peer model in the blockchain sense. So, academic (and other publishers) might be providing some other value functions, namely vouching for content quality. Publishers provide content curation, discovery, "findability," relevancy, advocacy, validation, and status ascribing, all of which might be useful attributes for content consumers. One way to improve a centralized model with blockchain technology is by applying an economy as a mechanism for making the incentives and reward structures of the system fairer.

Journalcoin could be issued as the token system of the publishing microeconomy to reward contributors, reviewers, editors, commentators, forum participants, advisors, staff, consultants, and indirect service providers involved in scientific publishing. This could help improve the quality and responsiveness of peer reviews, as reviews are published publicly, and reviewers are rewarded for their contribution. With Journalcoin, reviewers can receive reputational and remunerative rewards, and more transparency and exchange is created between authors, reviewers, and the scientific community and public. ElsevierJournalcoin and SpringerJournalcoin, for example, could be issued as metacoins, running on top of the Bitcoin blockchain, say as Counterparty assets, fully convertible at any time to Bitcoin or other cryptocurrencies.

A token-based coin such as Researchcoin could be used for individuals to collectively indicate interest and purchase the rights to read a certain research paper that is otherwise buried behind a paywall. Medicinal Genomics envisions a multisig, Bitcoin-based voting system for the public to indicate their demand to open source scientific papers related to pandemic disease (which the public ironically funds in the first place with tax dollars, yet cannot access).[153] For example, individuals with a mutation in the NPC1 gene have been found to be resistant to Ebola infection.[154] This kind of information could be easily used by empowered biocitizens to look up in their own personalized genomic data to see if they have higher conferred resistance to Ebola or other diseases such as HIV, which also has higher resistance in individuals with certain genotypes.[155] Although some are in favor of individuals having access to their own data, others feel that they may read too much into it without appropriate medical counsel. The Alzheimer's disease study mentioned previously, however, does hint that the benefits seem to outweigh the costs.

Related to Journalcoin, ExperimentalResultscoin could be another idea, implemented in the context of science journals, to incentivize and reward science experiment replications (helping to solve the problem of the 80 percent irreplicability of scientific experimental results), the publishing of negative results and raw data (just 45 percent are willing to make this available), and counter other biases in scientific publishing, such as priming, duplicate results, and carelessness.[156]

Just as Bitcoin is a digital payment mechanism for transactions between humans but could also empower the machine economy in machine-to-machine (M2M) and Internet of Things (IoT) payments, ExperimentalResultscoin could likewise serve as a mechanism for incentives, coordination, and tracking science executed by both humans and machines. Increasingly, both robotic lab aides and algorithmic programs are facilitating and generating scientific discovery. Some examples include Lipson's computing algorithms that have distilled physical laws from experimental data,[157] Muggleton's microfluidic robot scientist,[158] and Waltz and Buchanan's AI scientific partners.[159]

The 3.0 sense of applying blockchain technology to publishing would be having the blockchain completely fulfill the functions of the publisher (like a "semantic Verisign," vouching mechanism for qualitative content). A DAO/DAC/AI/VM model might be able to use data-based metrics (like the number of reads both in general and by affinity peers or colleagues, the number of comments, semantic keyword matching, and concept matching) to determine targeted content of quality and interest. The micropayment aspect of the blockchain could be used to make this a fee-based service. The idea is semantic peer-to-peer search, integrating the social networking layer (to identify peers) and adding blockchain economic and privacy functionality. Automatic nonpeer, nonhuman content-importance ascription models might also be a possibility.

Another means of employing the blockchain in academic publishing could be using it for plagiarism detection and avoidance, or better, for autocitation (an Ethereum smart contract/DAO that does a literature search and automatically cites all related work would be a tremendous time-saver). This could be accomplished through off-chain indexed paper storage repositories linking the asset by key to the blockchain. The blockchain could become the universal standard for the publication of papers, and of the underlying raw data and metadata files, essentially creating a universal cataloging system and library for research papers. Blockchain economics could make digital asset purchase of the papers easier by assigning every paper a Bitcoin address (QR code) instead of requiring users to log in to publisher websites.

The Blockchain Is Not for Every Situation

Despite the many interesting potential uses of blockchain technology, one of the most important skills in the developing industry is to see where it is and is not appropriate to use cryptocurrency and blockchain models. Not all processes need an economy or a payments system, or peer-to-peer exchange, or decentralization, or robust public record keeping. Further, the scale of operations is a relevant factor, because it might not make sense to have every tiny microtransaction recorded on a public blockchain; for example, blog-post tip-jar transactions could be batched into sidechains in which one overall daily transaction is recorded. Sidechains are more broadly proposed as an infrastructural mechanism by which multiblock chain ecosystems can exchange and transfer assets.[160] Especially with M2M/IoT device-to-device communication, there are many open questions about the most effective ways to incorporate market principles (if at all) to coordinate resources, incentivize certain goal-directed behavior, and have tracking and payments remuneration. Even before we consider the potential economic models for M2M/IoT payments, we must work out general coordination protocols for how large swarms of devices can communicate, perhaps deploying control system and scheduling software for these machine social networks, adding new layers of communication protocols like a "chirp" for simple microcommunications such as on, off, start, and stop.[161]

In the farther future, different classes of blockchains for different kinds of applications could be optimized. Maybe there could be daily purchase blockchains for the grocery store and coffee shop purchases, and others for large-ticket items like real estate and automobiles. More stridently different functionality is needed for noneconomic-market blockchains, for government services, intellectual property registration, notary services, science activities, and health-record keeping. The key question is distinguishing the economic principles needed for the different range of functions with which blockchain technology could be helpful. However, not every operation is one of value registration and exchange.

Not all of the ideas described need a blockchain; they do not require sequential, public, and distributed data storage. They could instead be implemented through other technology such as cloud storage or distributed computing models more generally. However, blockchain technology could be included to provide additional functionality, and further, it is not possible at present to see all of the potential future benefits and uses of blockchain technology that might emerge.

Another reason that the blockchain is not for every situation is because we do not want to "economify" everything. We do not want to reduce the qualitative aspects of life to a purely and nakedly economic situation. The idea of a remunerative coin accompanying many more situations and making the economics of situations more explicit is welcome in some ways but repugnant in others. However, the broader conceptualization of economy evoked by blockchain technology invites a new consideration of the notions of transfer, exchange, and acknowledgment that is deeply qualitative and could persist even as blockchain-enabled features do not (and should not) become omnipresent.

Centralization-Decentralization Tension and Equilibrium

There is a mix of forces both toward centralization and decentralization operating in the blockchain industry. In fact, it is the blockchain that has defined the landscape of models to comprise those that are both centralized and decentralized. Aside from the Internet, there have not been many large-scale standardized decentralization models that have been readily conceptualized and used in different contexts to organize activity. Even though decentralization is the core enabling functionality of blockchain technology (the decentralized trustless cryptographic transaction recording system and public ledger), there are also many centralization pressures. One is the centralization forces toward developing the standard plumbing layers of the blockchain economy. The Bitcoin blockchain has 90 percent cryptocurrency market capitalization, and some projects consider it safest and easiest to build protocol 3.0 ideas on this installed base without having to mount a mining operation on a new altcoin blockchain. Mining is another area upon which there are many centralization pressures. The fierce competition has driven mining from individuals with mining rigs to mining pools and custom ASICs such that a few large mining pools register most of the new Bitcoin blocks and have started to reach the 51 percent threshold of controlled hash power, which could result in a mining takeover. It remains to be seen how forces toward economic efficiency through centralization and trustless exchange through decentralization will come to equilibrium.

CHAPTER 5

Advanced Concepts

Terminology and Concepts

The blockchain economy is triggering the invention of many new ideas and the reappropriation of existing concepts and terminology in innovative ways. It prompts investigating the definition of terms that have been taken for granted and passed unquestioned for years, such as *money, currency, property, government, sovereignty,* and *intellectual property.* The questioning of underlying definitions and the reappropriation of terms position these concepts more openly and accessibly for application to current situations. Blockchain-related concepts are more actively in people's minds and ready to apply at the generalized level. For example, consider a library. At the more generalized conceptual level, a library is a system of value exchange; there are product and service offerings, like books and research, being taken up by those with whom the value proposition resonates. New models like blockchain technology force us to consider reality at the more generalized level of the concepts behind a specific instantiation. This leads us to imagine other specific situations that could be realized with those concepts. For example, a blockchain is a technology for decentralization. Bitcoin is the instantiation of decentralization as a digital currency, but decentralization could be instantiated in many ways, such as smart property, delegate democracy governance services, and community-based credit bureaus. In short, we start to see the world of possibility, or the world *as* possibility, as French philosopher Deleuze would say.[162] Further, we need to have tools for realizing this possibility; in the generalized conceptualization process, blockchain-related concepts become ready at hand or available to us, as Heidegger would say.[163]

In this fomentive environment, we can more easily create new conceptssuch as GoTo-Lunchcoin or Whatevercoin, applying a fuller conceptualization of *coin* in the cryptocurrency sense to a new situation. A coin or apptoken becomes a signifier that facilitates some application. I as a community member have earned some coin or token by performing some service like mining (transaction ledger administration) or via crowdfunding that I can burn, spend, or use in the network to acquire or consume something of value. In this sense, GoToLunchcoin is earned free time from work completed in the morning that can now be spent in refreshing and re-energizing. The economic principle of a cycle of resources expended and replenished is invoked. In this more elemental mode of concept generation, we can more immediately and intuitively understand the innovations of other ideas as we hear them. For example, if we heard of Precedentcoin in the legal setting, it would be easy to quickly intuit that it would likely be the apptoken or remunerative coin for performing the function of establishing precedents, and that there is probably some sort of new decentralized peer-based method for doing so.

New conceptualization can shift thinking back and forth between the levels of the general and the specific. An example of specific versus general thinking is the notion of an economy. An economy at the immediate, already-specified level is people buying and selling things, but at the higher, more generalized conceptual level, it is the production and consumption of things of value. Blockchain technology at the immediate, specified level is a decentralized public ledger for the recording of cryptocurrency transactions. Blockchain technology at the higher, more generalized conceptual level is a new class of thing like the Internet, a society's public records repository, a high-resolution tracking system for acknowledging human activity, a revolutionary organizing paradigm for human collaboration, an anticensorship mechanism, a liberty and equality enhancement tool, and a new organizing model for the discovery, transfer, and coordination of all quanta or discrete units of anything. These are just some of the things that blockchain technology is at this higher level. Comprehending blockchain technology at this more generalized level—with so many meanings of "what it is" conceptually—helps to demonstrate its significant potential impact.

Currency, Token, Tokenizing

Currency is just one idea that the cryptoeconomy is forcing us to rethink. One traditional dictionary definition of currency is "a system of money in general use in a particular country." This definition is already almost humorously and hopelessly outdated by Bitcoin's transnationality, not to mention that a "system of money" connotes centralized top-down issuance and sovereign control over money supplies. A secondary definition is perhaps more useful: "the quality or state of being used or accepted by many people." This claim is more applicable for cryptocurrencies, as we notice that although there is nothing backing Bitcoin like a gold standard, there is also nothing backing fiat currencies. What "backs" currency is the high adoption rate, being accepted by many people, the populace buying into the illusion of the concept of money. If more people were to accept the notion of cryptocurrencies and begin to use and trust them, they too could become as liquid as fiat currencies.

Just as the term *Bitcoin* can be used in a threefold manner to denote the underlying blockchain ledger, the Bitcoin transaction protocol, and the Bitcoin cryptocurrency, the term *currency* is being employed similarly to mean different things. In the cryptoeconomy context, one relevant way that the word *currency* is being used is in a generalized sense to connote "a unit of value that can be earned and used in a certain economic system," which is then likely to be fungibly tradable into other economic systems. The nomenclature *coin* could just as easily be *token*—that is, a digital token or access or tracking mechanism for different activities. There could be Appcoin, Communitycoin, Apptoken, or other terms all referring to different kinds of economic operations taking place within a community.

For example, the Counterparty currency (XCP) grants access to special features such as the ability to issue new assets, like a new appcoin, with the Counterparty protocol or economic system, that will be at any time convertible to XCP or Bitcoin, which is therefore convertible to USD, EUR, CNY, or any other fiat currency. Similarly, LTBcoin is a Counterparty-enabled coin issued by the Let's Talk Bitcoin media network to support its "local" economy. LTBcoin is used to transact incoming sponsorships, donations, and tips, and compensate outgoing listener rewards, community participation acknowledgment, content creation, reviews, and other forms of contribution. LTBcoin functions in the context of its own local economy, and is always immediately convertible to Bitcoin.[164] Other currencies could have similar use in their own local economies—"local" in the sense of interest community, not necessarily geography. In fact, one benefit of cryptocurrencies is their potential use as a tool for managing globally dispersed interest groups. Additionally, Communitycoin like the BoulderFarmersMarketcoin could provide additional features in its locality beyond just economic transactions, helping to build community cohesion and a more coordinated effort toward shared goals. Community cryptocoin could be a mechanism for increasing the resolution of interest group activities by being a more specific means of organizing and coordinating group behavior toward some goal.

Communitycoin: Hayek's Private Currencies Vie for Attention

The explosion of altcoin and Communitycoin, tokens or coins enabling economic function in a specific community context like the LTBcoin just described, suggests that some of the aspects of the world envisioned by Austrian School economist Friedrich Hayek might be coming to fruition. In *Denationalization of Money*, Hayek advocates a competitive private market for money instead of an arbitrary government monopoly.[165] He articulates other foundational thinking for the blockchain industry by arguing against Keynesian inflationary money in his essay *The "Paradox" of Savings*,[166] and points out the improved ability of vendors to respond in decentralized markets.[167] Regarding decentralized currency, Hayek posits a model in which financial institutions each issue their own currency and compete to maintain the value of their currencies through earnest productive activity.[168] There can be multiple concurrent currencies. This model could be deployed on a much wider basis in the blockchain economy, with the possibility that not just every financial institution, but every person, organization, and society, would issue their own currency or token (which could have a completely legitimate use within its locality and always be fungibly convertible to other currencies like Bitcoin). The idea would be to let a million currencies bloom; everyone could have their own coin, or multiple coins, just like everyone has their own blog, Twitter, and Instagram account. An example of this is Tatianacoin (*http://tatianamoroz.com/tatiana-coin/*), a musical artist coin issued by singer-songwriter Tatiana Moroz on the Counterparty protocol (*@tatianacoin*). Just as everyone became an author in the information revolution and their own personal health advocate in the genomic revolution, now everyone can become their own banker in the blockchain revolution. Some groups of currencies could and should compete, whereas other classes of currencies could coexist cooperatively as complements in discrete and separate venues.

Campuscoin

Some of the most obvious communities with their own economies for which currency issuance makes sense are business and university campuses. There should be an open source, templated solution for any university (administrators and student groups alike) to easily issue Campuscoin (e.g., ASUcoin). The same templated altcoin issuance could extend to groups within these communities, like DeltaChiCoin or NeuroscienceConferenceCoin, to support any specific group's activities. The Campuscoin issuance template could have specific prepackaged modules. First, there could be a module for buying and selling assets within the local community, an OpenBazaar- or Craigslist-like asset exchange module. Second, there could be a sharing economy module, a decentralized model of Airbnb for dorm rooms, Getaround for transportation including cars and bikes, and LaZooz peer-based ride sharing. Third, there could be a consulting or "advisory services" module for all manner of advice, mentoring, coaching, and tutoring related to classes, departments, majors, and careers. Recent graduates could earn Campuscoin by consulting to job-seeking seniors with specific services like advice and mock interviews; freshmen could provide counsel to high school seniors; and former students in a class could provide advice to current students. Campuscoin could provide a remunerative mechanism for these activities, which have been supplied on a volunteer basis and thus have been scarce where they could be abundant. By providing remuneration and acknowledgment, Campuscoin could provide a much more dynamic and connected network of those who have had similar experiences. In addition to remunerative economics, Campuscoin can be used to connect communities. A fourth module could be a "peer-to-peer learning network" for notes sharing, book sharing (solving the problem that a certain book is checked out until the end of the term), finding team members, forming study groups, studying for tests, and providing other kinds of support. Fifth, there could be a RealJobs module connecting local employers with students for topical internships and jobs with industry exposure and job force readiness training, all in a rewards-structured environment.

There are several efforts under way to support students learning about and using cryptocurrencies on university campuses. The student-founded Campus Cryptocurrency Network (*http://collegecrypto.org/*) counts 150 clubs in its network as of September 2014 and is a primary resource for students interested in starting campus cryptocurrency clubs. In the future, this network could be the standard repository for templated Campuscoin applications. Likewise, students founded and operate the *Bit coin Association of Berkeley* (*http://bitcoin.berkeley.edu/*) and organized their first hackathon in November 2014. MIT, with the MIT Bitcoin Project (*http://mitbitcoin project.org/*), has made a significant commitment to encourage the use and awareness of cryptocurrency among students, and it plans to give half a million dollars' worth of Bitcoin to undergraduates. Students were invited to claim their $100 of Bitcoin per person in October 2014.[169] Stanford University has made an effort to develop cryptography courses (*https://github.com/SymbolicSystems150*), which it offers for free online.

Coin Drops as a Strategy for Public Adoption

The MIT Bitcoin Project is effectively a coin drop, the simultaneous distribution of Bitcoin to entire populations to spur mainstream learning, trust, and adoption. A similar but larger-scale coin drop, the BitDrop, is scheduled for the Caribbean island nation of Dominica for March 14, 2015, as part of the Pi Day mathematical festival. Bitcoin will be sent by SMS via Coinapult to all 70,000 residents.[170] The goal is to create the world's largest and highest density Bitcoin community. The project began as a brainstorming exercise to facilitate adoption and put Bitcoin into the hands of as many people as possible. Dominica was chosen as optimal because the country has a relatively small population, a high cellular telephony penetration rate, and a position as a regional education center, and it is the center of an active intraisland, intracurrency trade and remittance economy. Bitcoin ATMs and merchant point-of-sale (POS) systems are to be installed as part of the project to help foster ongoing use of Bitcoin after the coin drop.

Coin drops or airdrops have been used in other situations; for example, "Nationcoin" has been used to shore up national identity. Iceland targeted residents with free cryptocurrency in the Auroracoin project (*http://auroracoin.org/*), and similar efforts include Scotcoin (*http://scotcoin.org/*), Spaincoin, and Greececoin, although there does not appear to have been a high degree of ongoing activity with these Nationcoin cryptocurrencies.[171] One reason that Ecuador banned Bitcoin was because it plans to launch its own national cryptocurrency.[172] Nationcoin could help bolster a sentiment of national patrimony, especially as many Eurozone nations have suffered from European Central Bank regulation impositions as a result of participating in the Euro. The same kind of Nationcoin benefits could be available in the idea of Tribecoin as the patrimony-supporting coin issuance of native peoples. The Pine Ridge Indian Reservation in South Dakota was the first American Indian tribe to launch its own cryptocurrency, MazaCoin, using the tribal nation's sovereignty to set its own rules on cryptocurrencies.[173]

Currency: New Meanings

The key point is that the term *currency* could begin to mean different things in the cryptoeconomy context, especially much more than in the basic *money* sense of serving as a payment mechanism for goods and services. A second important sense of the word *currency* in the cryptoeconomy context is emerging as "something of value that can be usefully deployed in some situation," or, as described previously, "a unit of value that can be earned and used in a certain economic system." There is the general idea of a token, currency, or appcoin allowing access to certain features of an economic system. Having Bitcoin, for example, allows access to performing transactions on the blockchain. Privileges are accorded to users in some cases just by their holding Bitcoin, as this confirms ownership, and in other cases by their actually spending the Bitcoin. Considering currency more broadly in these ways starts to widen its applicability to many other situations. A currency is a token of value that can be earned and deployed. A currency stores value and is transmissible. This generalized definition supports the claim that there can be many nonmonetary currencies that are conceived in the same structure. For example, reputation is a unit of value that can be earned and deployed in certain situations; it is a nonmonetary currency in the sense that it is a proxy for status or some kinds of tasks that a person can do. Likewise, health is a commodity of value that may be earned and can be deployed in specific situations. This broader notion of currency as an earnable and deployable commodity extends to many other nonmonetary currencies beyond reputation and health, such as intention, attention, time, ideas, and creativity.

Currency Multiplicity: Monetary and Nonmonetary Currencies

Altcoin multiplicity is just one venue of currency multiplicity in the modern world. More broadly, we are living in an increasingly multicurrency society with all kinds of monetary and nonmonetary currencies. First, there is currency multiplicity in the sense of monetary currency in that there are many different fiat currencies (USD, CNY, EUR, GBP, etc.). Second, there are many other nonfiat, non-blockchain-based currencies like loyalty points and airline miles; one estimate is that there are 4,000 such altcurrencies.[174] Now there is also a multiplicity of blockchain-based cryptocurrencies like Bitcoin, Litecoin, and Dogecoin. Beyond monetary currencies, there is currency multiplicity in nonmonetary currencies too (as just discussed), such as reputation, intention, and attention.[175]

Market principles have been employed to develop metrics for measuring nonmonetary currencies such as influence, reach, awareness, authenticity, engagement, action taking, impact, spread, connectedness, velocity, participation, shared values, and presence.[176] Now, blockchain technology could make these nonmonetary social currencies more trackable, transmissible, transactable, and monetizable. Social networks could become social economic networks. For example, reputation as one of the most recognizable nonmonetary currencies has always been an important intangible asset, but was not readily monetizable other than indirectly as an attribute of labor capital. However, social network currencies can now become transactable with web-based cryptocurrency tip jars (like Reddcoin) and other micropayment mechanisms that were not previously feasible or transnationally scalable with traditional fiat currency. Just as collaborative work projects such as open source software development can become more acknowledgeable and remunerable with GitHub commits and line-item contribution tracking, cryptocurrency tip jars can provide a measurable record and financial incentive for contribution-oriented online activities. One potential effect of this could be that if market principles were to become the norm for intangible resource allocation and exchange, all market agents might begin to have a more intuitive and pervasive sense and demonstration of exchange and reciprocity. Thus, social benefits such as a more collaborative society could be a result of what might initially seem to be only a deployment of economic principles.

Demurrage Currencies: Potentially Incitory and Redistributable

Currency is one such core concept in blockchain technology that is being stretched, extended, and reunderstood: currency as a digital token, a facilitation mechanism for quantized transfer. Within the notion of currency is the idea of a *demurrage currency*. *Demurrage* means carrying cost—that is, the cost to carry an asset. The term originated in the freight and shipping industry to indicate the extra charge or cost associated with the detention in port of a vessel by the ship owner, as in loading or unloading, beyond the time allowed or agreed upon. In the cryptocurrency sense, demurrage can mean being deflationary (value losing) over time, thus incitory (stimulatory) in that it incites some form of action taking (i.e.; spending) in the shorter term to realize value before it is lost. The currency itself thus encourages economic activity. Demurrage, then, is the compact concept of an attribute, the idea of an automatic motivating or incitory property being built in to something. Further, another aspect of demurrage currencies (or really all digital network–based asset allocation, tracking, interaction, and transaction structures) is the notion of periodic automatic redistribution of the currency (the resource) across all network nodes at certain prespecified times, or in the case of certain events. Demurrage features could become a powerful and standard currency administration tool.

Freicoin and Healthcoin are two examples of uses of a demurrage currency with a built-in mechanism for action taking in the form of spending. Demurrage currencies might be ideal for the implementation of *Guaranteed Basic Income initiatives* (GBIs), systems whereby all citizens or residents of a country would regularly receive an allowance—a sum of money sufficient to meet basic living expenses. GBIcoin or Freicoin could be a straightforward currency for basic living expenses that runs out or resets on a periodic basis such as weekly, monthly, or annually to keep the system streamlined and efficient without artificial overhangs created by hoarding. The money would be more like a coupon, expiring after certain amounts of time. The currency loses value, so the incentive is to spend it or just not use it.

A GBIcoin like Freicoin would likely not be the only currency, but would be a special-use currency, like Healthcoin, and would exist in the context of a Hayekian complementary or multicurrency society. This is the idea of having multiple currencies (not just multiple asset classes), but different currencies for different purposes. The Freicoin Cashcoin might be like a debit card for short-term consumable basic living expenditures. Spending could be in one coin and savings in another. Different classes of coins could have features adapted to specific contexts for savings, investment, and real estate transactions, and so on. The concept of GBIcoin or Freicoin is essentially a Spendcoin, Cashcoin, or Debitcoin that could be denominated in the basic national currency (Nationcoin) like UScoin or Americoin for supporting basic day-to-day living expenses, or perhaps more administratively efficient at the state level in Statecoin, like NYcoin.

More broadly, complementary currency systems and multicurrency systems are just the application of the same phenomenon that has been used to reinvent many other areas of modern life. Multicurrency systems are the granularification of currency, finance, and money; the seemingly infinite explosion of long-tail power-law personalization and choice making that has come to coffee (Starbucks), books and movies (Amazon, Netflix), information (blogs, Twitter), learning (YouTube, MOOCs), and relationships (polyamory). Now is merely the advent of these various systems of personalized multiplicity coming to money and finance.

Healthcoin could be similarly conceived as a demurrage currency. Health-services spending could be denominated in Healthcoin. In the United States, many health plans such as Health Savings Accounts (HSAs) and Cafeteria Plans are already demurrage currencies in that they are set up to expire each year. The system resets, so strange bubbles and artificialities are not introduced. All national health services could be denominated and paid in Healthcoin.

In addition to the potential value loss and therefore "incentive to spend" aspect of a demurrage currency, another feature of a demurrage currency, which could be a feature of any cryptocurrency, is the possibility of periodic redistribution across network nodes. This also incentivizes currency holders to spend out the currency. At the more extreme end, and as an indication of connecting currency operations to policy objectives, this feature could provide the means for a society to periodically redistribute income across the populace.

An obvious limitation of managed demurrage currency systems is that because enterprising human agents are the constituents, it is likely, if incentives were not aligned, that they would find all manner of clever mechanisms and loopholes to circumvent the system—for example, to get around the antihoarding property of a demurrage currency if there were some benefit or perceived benefit to hoarding. However, the goal would be to appropriately align incentives, and really to move into a world in which circumvention incentives would be irrelevant because the currency distribution system would be able to meet the panoply of personalized needs a society has with money for basic expenditure. The certainty of GBIcoin, Freicoin, or Cashcoin reissuance in subsequent time periods, assuming not inconsequentially that the system is stable and that there is trust in the system, could create a mindset of abundance, which together with the demurrage or value-losing aspect of the currency obviates the need for hoarding and antiscarcity measures. This would be a conceptualization of money and the means of meeting basic survival needs that is unprecedented in human history—a trustable source of having basic needs met such that individuals do not even have to think about this. The great potential benefit of having basic survival needs met could be that it might usher in not just an era of abundance, but also free up human cognitive surplus to work on other higher-order interests, challenges, and concerns, thus architecting a new era of human society, collaboration, and productivity.[177]

Extensibility of Demurrage Concept and Features

The action-incitory and dynamic redistribution features of a demurrage currency are not just useful for developing special-purpose currencies in a multicurrency society, but, like many blockchain concepts, potentially extensible on a much broader basis beyond the context of currency, economics, and financial systems. The presupposition is that many things are in some way a currency, an economy, or a network, and that we are living in an increasingly multicurrency society, literally for monetary systems and also in the sense of currency, reputation, intention, attention, and ideas as currency.

In this framework, we can see that Fitbit and smartwatch are demurrage health currencies. A demurrage currency is an action-inciting currency, a stimulatory currency, because it gets you to do something. Fitbit is a demurrage (action-inciting) health currency, a currency that prompts you to take action. The demurrage (incitory) mechanism is that perhaps in the evening, you see a notification on your Fitbit or smartwatch telling you that you have taken 19,963 steps today, thus encouraging you to reach 20,000; the way that Fitbit and smartwatch present information is a demurrage mechanism that encourages you to take action. Thus, health as a demurrage currency can be used as a design principle in developing technology to facilitate action taking that is in the interest of the agent.

The dynamic redistribution property of the demurrage concept can also be applied to many other contexts, such as when resources are distributed across networks. Networks are an increasingly pervasive feature of the modern world. A clear use case for the demurrage dynamic redistribution feature is in the case of resource allocation through automatic networks or tradenets. Here, more efficient, larger, more scalable, more trackable systems are sought for the distribution of consumable resources like gas and electricity, transportation quanta (i.e., Uber/LaZooz, self-driving vehicles, or automated pod transport systems envisioned in the farther future), clean water, food, health-care services, relief aid, crisis-response supplies, and even emotional support or mental-performance coaching (for individuals permissioned in consumer EEG rigs). This is the idea of using the demurrage concept in other network systems to dynamically, automatically redistribute resources for optimization. The concept is combining networks and demurrage currency to enable new functionality like dynamic automatic redistribution across network nodes and enable the predictive and on-demand smart clustering of resources where needed. Some examples are predicting and delivering an increased load of Ubers and cabs to the airport when more flights are due to arrive, and preparing available electricity units on hotter days and fuel oil units on colder days. This is the idea of automatic resource redistribution in smart networks, possible using demurrage as a design element.

There are other examples of deploying the demurrage concept in smart networks. Health is itself a network and a demurrage currency; an earnable and spendable commodity; a linked, continually autoredistributing enabler operating fractally at multiple organizational levels, among synapses, cells, organisms/humans, and societies. We can start to see the body and brain as a Dapp, DAO, or DAC where already many systems are automatically operating at the unconscious level, and where more systems like cognitive enhancement, preventive medicine, and pathology treatment could be explicitly managed with Dapp AI systems. This concept combines a demurrage resource-allocation system with a Dapp, enabling the functionality of the automatic redistribution of any resource commodity within a system. This could be useful, for example, in the case of neural potentiation in a brain, increasing nerve impulses along pathways, for which systemwide resource redistribution could optimize performance. We want to redistribute and equalize potentiation capability among synapses in a physical brain with our cognitive enhancement technology or in an artificial intelligence or software-simulated brain. Different kinds of brain-based resources— such as potentiation capability, optogenetic excitation (manipulating living cells with inserted genetically adapted proteins and light), or transcranial direct stimulation— could be the demurrage currencies targeted for redistribution across a brain or mind-file. Another example of demurrage redistribution in the health context could be for cellular resources such as oxygen, waste removal nanobots, and circulating lab-on-chips as the physical enablement currencies of the body. Likewise, ideas could be the redistributable currency of collaborative teams, and liberty, trust, and compassion the currency of society. Bitcoin is already effectuated as a demurrage currency and smart network resource allocation mechanism in the sense of redistributing the currency of liberty across society.

CHAPTER 6

Limitations

The blockchain industry is still in the early stages of development, and there are many different kinds of potential limitations. The classes of limitations are both internal and external, and include those related to technical issues with the underlying technology, ongoing industry thefts and scandals, public perception, government regulation, and the mainstream adoption of technology.

Technical Challenges

A number of technical challenges related to the blockchain, whether a specific one or the model in general, have been identified.

The issues are in clear sight of developers, with different answers to the challenges posited, and avid discussion and coding of potential solutions. Insiders have different degrees of confidence as to whether and how these issues can be overcome to evolve into the next phases of blockchain industry development. Some think that the de facto standard will be the Bitcoin blockchain, as it is the incumbent, with the most widely deployed infrastructure and such network effects that it cannot help but be the standardized base. Others are building different new and separate blockchains (like Ethereum) or technology that does not use a blockchain (like Ripple). One central challenge with the underlying Bitcoin technology is scaling up from the current maximum limit of 7 transactions per second (the VISA credit card processing network routinely handles 2,000 transactions per second and can accommodate peak volumes of 10,000 transactions per second), especially if there were to be mainstream adoption of Bitcoin.[178] Some of the other issues include increasing the block size, addressing blockchain bloat, countering vulnerability to 51 percent mining attacks, and implementing hard forks (changes that are not backward compatible) to the code, as summarized here:[179]

Throughput

The Bitcoin network has a potential issue with throughput in that it is processing only one transaction per second (tps), with a theoretical current maximum of 7 tps. Core developers maintain that this limit can be raised when it becomes necessary. One way that Bitcoin could handle higher throughput is if each block were bigger, though right now that leads to other issues with regard to size and blockchain bloat. Comparison metrics in other transaction processing networks are VISA (2,000 tps typical; 10,000 tps peak), Twitter (5,000 tps typical; 15,000 tps peak), and advertising networks (>100,000 tps typical).

Latency

Right now, each Bitcoin transaction block takes 10 minutes to process, meaning that it can take at least 10 minutes for your transaction to be confirmed. For sufficient security, you should wait more time—about an hour—and for larger transfer amounts it needs to be even longer, because it must outweigh the cost of a double-spend attack (in which Bitcoins are double-spent in a separate transaction before the merchant can confirm their reception in what appears to be the intended transaction). Again, as the comparison metric, VISA takes seconds at most.

Size and bandwidth

The blockchain is 25 GB, and grew by 14 GB in the last year. So it already takes a long time to download (e.g., 1 day). If throughput were to increase by a factor of 2,000 to VISA standards, for example, that would be 1.42 PB/year or 3.9 GB/day. At 150,000 tps, the blockchain would grow by 214 PB/year. The Bitcoin community calls the size problem "bloat," but that assumes that we want a small blockchain; however, to really scale to mainstream use, the blockchain would need to be big, just more efficiently accessed. This motivates centralization, because it takes resources to run the full node, and only about 7,000 servers worldwide (*https://getaddr.bitnodes.io/*) do in fact run full Bitcoind nodes, meaning the Bitcoin daemon (the full Bitcoin node running in the background). It is being discussed whether locations running full nodes should be compensated with rewards. Although 25 GB of data is trivial in many areas of the modern "big data" era and data-intensive science with terabytes of data being the standard, this data can be compressed, whereas the blockchain cannot for security and accessibility reasons. However, perhaps this is an opportunity to innovate new kinds of compression algorithms that would make the blockchain (at much larger future scales) still usable, and storable, while retaining its integrity and accessibility. One innovation to address blockchain bloat and make the data more accessible is APIs, like those from Chain (*https://chain.com/*) and other vendors, that facilitate automated calls to the full Bitcoin blockchain. Some of the operations are to obtain address balances and balances changes, and notify user applications when new transactions or blocks are created on the network. Also, there are web-based block explorers (like *https://blockchain.info/*), middleware applications allowing partial queries of blockchain data, and frontend customer-facing mobile ewallets with greatly streamlined blockchain data.

Security

There are some potential security issues with the Bitcoin blockchain. The most worrisome is the possibility of a 51-percent attack, in which one mining entity could grab control of the blockchain and double-spend previously transacted coins into his own account.[180] The issue is the centralization tendency in mining where the competition to record new transaction blocks in the blockchain has meant that only a few large mining pools control the majority of the transaction recording. At present, the incentive is for them to be good players, and some (like Ghash.io) have stated that they would not take over the network in a 51-percent attack, but the network is insecure.[181] Double-spending might also still be possible in other ways—for example, spoofing users to resend transactions, allowing malicious coders to double-spend coins. Another security issue is that the current cryptography standard that Bitcoin uses, Elliptic Curve Cryptography, might be crackable as early as 2015; however, financial cryptography experts have proposed potential upgrades to address this weakness.[182]

Wasted resources

Mining draws an enormous amount of energy, all of it wasted. The earlier estimate cited was $15 million per day, and other estimates are higher.[183] On one hand, it is the very wastefulness of mining that makes it trustable—that rational agents compete in an otherwise useless proof-of-work effort in hopes of the possibility of reward—but on the other hand, these spent resources have no benefit other than mining.

Usability

The API for working with Bitcoind (the full node of all code) is far less user-friendly than the current standards of other easy-to-use modern APIs, such as widely used REST APIs.

Versioning, hard forks, multiple chains

Some other technical issues have to do with the infrastructure. One issue is the proliferation of blockchains, and that with so many different blockchains in existence, it could be easy to deploy the resources to launch a 51-percent attack on smaller chains. Another issue is that when chains are split for administrative or versioning purposes, there is no easy way to merge or cross-transact on forked chains.

Another significant technical challenge and requirement is that a full ecosystem of plug-and-play solutions be developed to provide the entire value chain of service delivery. For example, linked to the blockchain there needs to be secure decentralized storage (MaidSafe, Storj), messaging, transport, communications protocols, namespace and address management, network administration, and archival. Ideally, the blockchain industry would develop similarly to the cloud-computing model, for which standard infrastructure components—like cloud servers and transport systems—were defined and implemented very quickly at the beginning to allow the industry to focus on the higher level of developing value-added services instead of the core infrastructure. This is particularly important in the blockchain economy due to the sensitive and complicated cryptographic engineering aspects of decentralized networks. The industry is sorting out exactly how much computer network security, cryptography, and mathematics expertise the average blockchain startup should have—ideally not much if they can rely on a secure infrastructure stack on which this functionality already exists. That way, the blockchain industry's development can be hastened, without every new business having to reinvent the wheel and worry about the fact that its first customer-facing ewallet was not multisig (or whatever the current industry standard is, as cryptographic security standards will likely continue to iterate).

Some of the partial proposed solutions to the technical issues discussed here are as follows:

Offline wallets to store the majority of coins
Different manner of offline wallets could be used to store the bulk of consumer cryptocoins—for example, paper wallets, cold storage, and bit cards (*http://www.bit-card.de/*).

Dark pools
There could be a more granular value chain such that big crypto-exchanges operate their own internal databases of transactions, and then periodically synchronize a summary of the transactions with the blockchain—an idea borrowed from the banking industry.

Alternative hashing algorithms
Litecoin and other cryptocurrencies use scrypt, which is at least slightly faster than Bitcoin, and other hashing algorithms could be innovated.

Alternatives to proof of work for Byzantine consensus
There are   many other consensus models proposed—such as proof of stake, hybrids, and variants—that have lower latency, require less computational power, waste fewer resources, and improve security for smaller chains. Consensus without mining is another area being explored, such as in Tendermint's modified version of DLS (the solution to the Byzantine Generals' Problem by Dwork, Lynch, and Stockmeyer), with bonded coins belonging to byzantine participants.[184] Another idea for consensus without mining or proof of work is through a consensus algorithm such as Hyperledger's (*http://www.hyperledger.com*), which is based on the Practical Byzantine Fault Tolerance algorithm.

Only focus on the most recent or unspent outputs
Many blockchain operations could be based on surface calculations of the most recent or unspent outputs, similar to how credit card transactions operate. "Thin wallets" operate this way, as opposed to querying a full Bitcoind node, and this is how Bitcoin ewallets work on cellular telephones. A related proposal is Cryptonite (*http://www.cryptonite.info*), which has a "mini-blockchain" abbreviated data scheme.

Blockchain interoperability

To coordinate transactions between blockchains, there are several side chains projects proposed, such as those by Blockstream (*http://www.blockstream.com*).

Posting bond deposits

The security of proposed alternative consensus mechanisms like Tendermints's DLS protocol (which requires no proof-of-work mining) could be reinforced with structural elements such as requiring miners to post bond deposits to blockchains. This could help resolve the security issue of the "nothing at stake in short time ranges" problem, where malicious players (before having a stake) could potentially fork the blockchain and steal cryptocurrency in a double-spend attack.[185] Bond deposits could be posted to blockchains like Tendermint does, making it costly to fork and possibly improving operability and security.

REST APIs

Essentially secure calls in real time, these could be used in specific cases to help usability. Many blockchain companies provide alternative wallet interfaces that have this kind of functionality, such as Blockchain.info's numerous wallet APIs.

Business Model Challenges

Another noted challenge, both functional and technical, is related to business models. At first traditional business models might not seem applicable to Bitcoin since the whole point of decentralized peer-to-peer models is that there are no facilitating intermediaries to take a cut/transaction fee (as in one classical business model). However, there are still many worthwhile revenue-generating products and services to provide in the new blockchain economy. Education and mainstream user-friendly tools are obvious low-hanging fruit (for example, being targeted by Coinbase, Circle Internet Financial, and Xapo), as is improving the efficiency of the entire worldwide existing banking and finance infrastructure like Ripple—another almost "no brainer" project, when blockchain principles are understood. Looking ahead, reconfiguring all of business and commerce with smart contracts in the Bitcoin 2.0 era could likely be complicated and difficult to implement, with many opportunities for service providers to offer implementation services, customer education, standard setting, and other value-added facilitations. Some of the many types of business models that have developed with enterprise software and cloud computing might be applicable, too, for the Bitcoin economy—for example, the Red Hat model (fee-based services to implement open source software), and SaaS, providing Software as a Service, including with customization. One possible job of the future could be smart contract auditor, to confirm that AI smart contracts running on the blockchain are indeed doing as instructed, and determining and measuring how the smart contracts have self-rewritten to maximize the issuing agent's utility.

Scandals and Public Perception

One of the biggest barriers to further Bitcoin adoption is its public perception as a venue for (and possible abettor of) the dark net's money-laundering, drug-related, and other illicit activity—for example, illegal goods online marketplaces such as Silk Road. Bitcoin and the blockchain are themselves neutral, as any technology, and are "dual use"; that is, they can be used for good or evil. Although there are possibilities for malicious use of the blockchain, the potential benefits greatly outweigh the potential downsides. Over time, public perception can change as more individuals themselves have ewallets and begin to use Bitcoin. Still, it must be acknowledged that Bitcoin as a pseudonymous enabler can be used to facilitate illegal and malicious activities, and this invites in-kind "Red Queen" responses (context-specific evolutionary arms races) appropriate to the blockchain. Computer virus detection software arose in response to computer viruses; and so far some features of the same constitutive technologies of Bitcoin (like Tor, a free and open software network) have been deployed back into detecting malicious players.

Another significant barrier to Bitcoin adoption is the ongoing theft, scandals, and scams (like so-called new altcoin "pump and dump" scams that try to bid up new altcoins to quickly profit) in the industry. The collapse of the largest Bitcoin exchange at the time, Tokyo-based MtGox, in March 2014 came to wide public attention. An explanation is still needed for the confusing irony that somehow in the blockchain, the world's most public transparent ledger, coins can disappear and still remain lost months later. The company said it had been hacked, and that the fraud was a result of a problem known as a "transaction malleability bug." The bug allowed malicious users to double-spend, transferring Bitcoins into their accounts while making MtGox think the transfer had failed and thus repeat the transactions, in effect transferring the value twice.[186] Analysts remain unsure if MtGox was an externally perpetrated hack or an internal embezzlement. The issue is that these kinds of thefts persist. For example, recent headlines inform us that the Moolah CEO disappeared with $1.4 million in Bitcoin (October 2014),[187] $2 million of Vericoin was stolen (July 2014),[188] and $620,000 was stolen in a Dogecoin mining attack (June 2014).[189]

Blockchain industry models need to solidify and mature such that there are better safeguards in place to stabilize the industry and allow both insiders and outsiders to distinguish between good and bad players. Oversight need not come from outside; congruently decentralized vetting, confirmation, and monitoring systems within the ecosystem could be established. An analogy from citizen science is realizing that oversight functions are still important, and reinforce the system by providing checks and balances. In DIYgenomics participant-organized research studies, for example, the oversight function is still fulfilled, but in some cases with a wholly new role relevant to the ecosystem—independent citizen ethicists—as opposed to traditional top-down overseers (in the form of a human-subjects research Institutional Review

Board).[190] Other self-regulating industries include movies, video games, and comic books.

There is the possibility that the entire blockchain industry could just collapse (either due to already prognosticated problems or some other factor as yet unforeseen). There is nothing to indicate that a collapse would be impossible. The blockchain economy does have a strong presence, as measured by diverse metrics such as coin market capitalizations (*http://coinmarketcap.com/*), investment in the sector, number of startups and people working in the sector, lines of GitHub code committed, and the amount of "newspaper ink" devoted to the sector. Already the blockchain industry is bigger and better established than the previous run at digital currencies (virtual-world currencies like the Second Life Linden dollar). However, despite the progress to date and lofty ideals of Bitcoin, maybe it is still too early for digital currency; maybe all of the right safeguards and structures are not yet in place for digital currencies to go fully mainstream (although Apple Pay, more than any other factor, may pave the way to full mainstream acceptance of digital currencies). Apple Pay could quite possibly be enough for the short term. It will be a long time before Bitcoin has the same user-friendly attributes of Apple Pay, such as latency of confirmation time.

Government Regulation

How government regulation unfolds could be one of the most significant factors and risks in whether the blockchain industry will flourish into a mature financial services industry. In the United States, there could be federal- and state-level legislation; deliberations continue into a second comment period regarding a much-discussed New York Bitlicense.[191] The New York Bitlicense could set the tone for worldwide regulation. On one hand, the Bitcoin industry is concerned about the extremely broad, wide-reaching, and extraterritorial language of the license as currently proposed. The license would encompass anyone doing anything with anyone else's Bitcoins, including basic wallet software (like the QT wallet).[192] However, on the other hand, regulated consumer protections for Bitcoin industry participants, like KYC (know your customer) requirements for money service businesses (MSBs), could hasten the mainstream development of the industry and eradicate consumer worry of the hacking raids that seem to plague the industry.

The deliberations and early rulings of worldwide governments on Bitcoin raise some interesting questions. One issue is the potential practical impossibility of carrying out taxation with current methods. A decentralized peer-to-peer sharing economy of Airbnb 2.0 and Uber 2.0 run on local implementations of OpenBazaar with individuals paying with cryptocurrencies renders traditional taxation structures impossible. The usual tracking and chokehold points to trace the consumption of goods and services might be gone. This has implications both for taxation and for the overall measurement of economic performance such as GDP calculations, which could have the beneficial impact of drawing populaces away from being overly and possibly incorrectly focused on consumption as a wellness metric. Instead, there could be an overhaul of the taxation system to a consumption-based tax on large-ticket visible items such as hard assets (cars, houses). Chokehold points would need to be easily visible for taxation, a "tax on sight" concept. A potential shift from an income tax–based system to a consumption tax–based system could be a significant change for societies.

A second issue that blockchain technology raises with regard to government regulation is the value proposition offered by governments and their business model. Some argue that in the modern era of big data, governments are increasingly unable to keep up with their record-keeping duties of recording and archiving information and making data easily accessible. On this view, governments could become obsolete because they cannot fund themselves the traditional way—by raising taxes. Blockchain technology could potentially help solve both of these challenges, and could at minimum supplement and help governments do their own jobs better, eventually making classes of government-provided services redundant. Recording all of a society's records on the blockchain could obviate the need for entire classes of public service. This view starkly paints governments as becoming redundant with the democratization of government features of the blockchain.

However, just as there might be both centralized and decentralized models to coordinate our activities in the world, there could likely be roles for both traditional government and new forms of blockchain-based government. There might still be a role for traditional centralized governments, but they will need to become economically rationalized, with real value propositions that resonate with constituencies, shrink costs, and demonstrate effectiveness. There could be hybrid governments in the future, like other industries, where automation is the forcing function, and the best "worker" for the job is a human/algorithmic pairing.[193] Perfunctory repetitive tasks are automated with blockchain registries and smart contracts, whereas government employees can move up the value chain.

Privacy Challenges for Personal Records

There are many issues to be resolved before individuals would feel comfortable storing their personal records in a decentralized manner with a pointer and possibly access via the blockchain. The potential privacy nightmare is that if all your data is online and the secret key is stolen or exposed, you have little recourse. In the current cryptocurrency architecture, there are many scenarios in which this might happen, just as today with personal and corporate passwords being routinely stolen or databases hacked—with broad but shallow consequences; tens of thousands of people deal with a usually minor inconvenience. If a thorough personal record is stolen, the implications could be staggering for an individual: identity theft to the degree that you no longer have your identity at all.

Overall: Decentralization Trends Likely to Persist

However, despite all of the potential limitations with the still-nascent blockchain economy, there is virtually no question that Bitcoin is a disruptive force and that its impact will be significant. Even if all of the current infrastructure developed by the blockchain industry were to disappear (or fall out of popularity, as virtual worlds have), much of their legacy could persist. The blockchain economy has provided new larger-scale ideas about how to do things. Even if you don't buy into the future of Bitcoin as a stable, long-term cryptocurrency, or blockchain technology as it is currently conceived and developing, there is a very strong case for decentralized models. Decentralization is an idea whose time has come. The Internet is large enough and liquid enough to accommodate decentralized models in new and more pervasive ways than has been possible previously. Centralized models were a good idea at the time, an innovation and revolution in human coordination hundreds of years ago, but now we have a new cultural technology, the Internet, and techniques such as distributed public blockchain ledgers that could facilitate activity to not only include all seven billion people for the first time, but also allow larger-scale, more complicated coordination, and speed our progress toward becoming a truly advanced society. If not the blockchain industry, there would probably be something else, and in fact there probably *will* be other complements to the blockchain industry anyway. It is just that the blockchain industry is one of the first identifiable large-scale implementations of decentralization models, conceived and executed at a new and more complex level of human activity.

CHAPTER 7

Conclusion

This book has tried to demonstrate that blockchain technology's many concepts and features might be broadly extensible to a wide variety of situations. These features apply not just to the immediate context of currency and payments (Blockchain 1.0), or to contracts, property, and all financial markets transactions (Blockchain 2.0), but beyond to segments as diverse as government, health, science, literacy, publishing, economic development, art, and culture (Blockchain 3.0), and possibly even more broadly to enable orders-of-magnitude larger-scale human progress.

Blockchain technology could be quite complementary in a possibility space for the future world that includes both centralized and decentralized models. Like any new technology, the blockchain is an idea that initially disrupts, and over time it could promote the development of a larger ecosystem that includes both the old way and the new innovation. Some historical examples are that the advent of the radio in fact led to increased record sales, and ereaders such as the Kindle have increased book sales. Now, we obtain news from the *New York Times*, blogs, Twitter, and personalized drone feeds alike. We consume media from both large entertainment companies and YouTube. Thus, over time, blockchain technology could exist in a larger ecosystem with both centralized and decentralized models.

There could be a large collection of both fiat currencies and cryptocurrencies existing side by side. In his book *Denationalization of Money*, economist Friedrich Hayek envisions complementary currencies competing for consumer attention. He saw multiple currencies at the level of financial institutions, but as everyone now has their own news outlets through their own blog, Twitter account, YouTube channel, and Instagram handle, so too could there be arbitrarily many cryptocurrencies, at the level of individuals or special interest groups and communities. Each of these cryptocurrencies could exist in its local economy, fully relevant and valid for value exchange and economic operation in that local context, like the Let's Talk Bitcoin community coin, musical artistÕs Tatianacoin, or community coin in your local farmers market, DIY maker lab, or school district. The local token would likely always be readily convertible out to more liquid cryptocurrencies and fiat currencies. This is the multiplicity and abundance property of blockchain technology. Blockchain technology could enable currency multiplicity in the form of many currencies potentially existing side by side, conceived with more granularity than fiat currencies, each for use in specific situations. The overall effect could be promoting a mindset of abundance as opposed to scarcity in regard to the concept of money, particularly if simultaneously accompanied by Guaranteed Basic Income (GBI) initiatives that covered basic survival needs for all individuals and thus enabled a higher-level cognitive focus. Currency could be reconceptualized in the context of what kinds of actions it enables in a community as opposed to exclusively being a means of obtaining and storing value.

The Blockchain Is an Information Technology

Perhaps most centrally, the blockchain is an information technology. But blockchain technology is also many other things. The blockchain as decentralization is a revolutionary new computing paradigm. The blockchain is the embedded economic layer the Web never had. The blockchain is the coordination mechanism, the line-item attribution, credit, proof, and compensation rewards tracking schema to encourage trustless participation by any intelligent agent in any collaboration. The blockchain "is a decentralized trust network."[194] The blockchain is Hayek's multiplicity of private complementary currencies for which there could be as many currencies as Twitter handles and blogs, all fully useful and accepted in their own hyperlocal contexts, and where Communitycoin issuance can improve the cohesion and actualization of any group. The blockchain is a cloud venue for transnational organizations. The blockchain is a means of offering personalized decentralized governance services, sponsoring literacy, and facilitating economic development. The blockchain is a tool that could prove the existence and exact contents of any document or other digital asset at a particular time. The blockchain is the integration and automation of human/machine interaction and the machine-to-machine (M2M) and Internet of Things (IoT) payment network for the machine economy. The blockchain and cryptocurrency is a payment mechanism and accounting system enabler for M2M communication. The blockchain is a worldwide decentralized public ledger for the registration, acknowledgment, and transfer of all assets and societal interactions, a society's public records bank, an organizing mechanism to facilitate large-scale human progress in previously unimagined ways. The blockchain is the technology and the system that could enable the global-scale coordination of seven billion intelligent agents. The blockchain is a consensus model at scale, and possibly the mechanism we have been waiting for that could help to usher in an era of friendly machine intelligence.

Blockchain AI: Consensus as the Mechanism to Foster "Friendly" AI

One forward-looking but important concern in the general future of technology is different ways in which artificial intelligence (AI) might arise and how to sponsor it such that it engenders a "friendly" or benevolent relationship with humans. There is the notion of a technological singularity, a moment when machine intelligence might supersede human intelligence. However, those in the field have not set forth any sort of robust plan for how to effect friendly AI, and many remain skeptical of this possibility.[195] It is possible that blockchain technology could be a useful connector of humans and machines in a world of increasingly autonomous machine activity through Dapps, DAOs, and DACs that might eventually give way to AI. In particular, consensus as a mechanism could be instrumental in bringing about and enforcing friendly AI.

Large Possibility Space for Intelligence

Speculatively looking toward the longer term, there might be a large possibility space of intelligence that includes humans, enhanced humans, different forms of human/ machine hybrids, digital mindfile uploads, and different forms of artificial intelligence like simulated brains and advanced machine learning algorithms. The blockchain as an information technology might be able to ease the future transition into a world with multiple kinds of machine, human, and hybrid intelligence. These intelligences would likely not be operating in isolation, but would be connected to communications networks. To achieve their goals, digital intelligences will want to conduct certain transactions over the network, many of which could be managed by blockchain and other consensus mechanisms.

Only Friendly AIs Are Able to Get Their Transactions Executed

One of the unforeseen benefits of consensus models might be that they could possibly enforce friendly AI, which is to say cooperative, moral players within a society.[196] In decentralized trust networks, an agentÕs reputation (where agents themselves remain pseudonymous) could be an important factor in whether his transactions will be executed, such that malicious players would not be able to get their transactions executed or recognized on the network. Any important transaction regarding resource access and use might require assent by consensus models. Thus, the way that friendly AI could be enforced is that even bad agents want to participate in the system to access resources and to do so, they need to look like good agents. Bad agents have to resemble good agents enough in reputation and behavior that they become indistinguishable from good agents because both behave well. A related example is that of sociopaths in real-life society who exist but are often transparent because they are forced into good player behavior through the structure and incentives of society. Of course, there are many possible objections to the idea that the blockchain structure could enforce friendly AI: bad agents might build their own smart networks for resource access, they might behave duplicitously while earning trust, and so on. This does not change the key point of seeing blockchain technology as a system of checks and balances for incentivizing and producing certain kinds of behavior while attempting to limit others. The idea is to create Occam's razor systems that are so useful in delivering benefits that it pays to play well, where the easiest best solution is to participate. Good player incentives are baked into the system.

Some of the key network operations that any digital intelligence might want to execute are secure access, authentication and validation, and economic exchange. Effectively, any network transaction that any intelligent agent cares about to conduct her goals will require some form of access or authentication that is consensus-signed, which cannot be obtained unless the agent has a good—which is to say benevolent—reputational standing on the network. This is how friendly AI might be effectuated in a blockchain consensus-based model.

Smart Contract Advocates on Behalf of Digital Intelligence

Not only could blockchain technology and consensus models be used potentially to obtain friendly AI behavior, the functionality might also be employed the other way around. For example, if you are an AI or a digitally uploaded human mindfile, smart contracts could possibly serve as your advocate in the future to confirm details about your existence and runtime environment. Another long-standing problem in AI has been that if you are a digital intelligence, how can you confirm your reality environment—that you still exist, that you are sufficiently backed up, that you are really running, and under what conditions? For example, you want to be sure that your data center has not shoved you onto an old DOS-based computer, or deleted you, or gone out of business. Smart contracts on the blockchain are exactly the kind of universal third-party advocate in future timeframes that could be used to verify and exercise control over the physical parameters of reality, of your existence as a digital intelligence. How it could work is that you would enact smart contracts on the blockchain to periodically confirm your runtime parameters and decentralized back-up copies. Smart contracts allow you to set up "future advocacy," a new kind of service that could have many relevant uses, even in the current practical sense of enforcing elder rights.

Speculatively, in the farther future, in advanced societies of billions of digital intelligences living and thriving in smart network systems, there would need to be sophisticated *oracles*, information arbiters accessed by blockchain smart contracts or some other mechanism. The business model could be "oracles as a service, a platform, or even as a public good." The Wikipedia of the future could be a blockchain-based oracle service to look up the current standard for digital mindfile processing, storage, and security, given that these standards would likely be advancing over time. "You are running on the current standard, Windows 36," your smart contract advocate might inform you. These kinds of mechanisms—dynamic oracle services accessible by smart contracts on universal public blockchains—could help to create a system of checks and balances within which digital intelligences or other nonembodied entities could feel comfortable not only in their survival, but also in their future growth.

Blockchain Consensus Increases the Information Resolution of the Universe

In closing, there is ample opportunity to explore more expansively the idea of the blockchain as an information technology, including what consensus models as a core feature might mean and enable. A key question is what is consensus-derived information; that is, what are its properties and benefits vis-à-vis other kinds of information? Is consensus-derived information a different kind or form of information? One way of conceiving of reality and the universe is as information flows. Blockchain technology helps call out that there are at least three different levels of information. Level one is dumb, unenhanced, unmodulated data. Level two could be posed as socially recommended data, data elements enriched by social network peer recommendation, which has been made possible by networked Internet models. The quality of the information is denser because it has been recommended by social peers. Now there is level three: blockchain consensus-validated data, data's highest yet recommendation level based on group consensus-supported accuracy and quality. Not just peer recommendations, but a formal structure of intelligent agent experts has formed a consensus about the quality and accuracy of this data. Blockchain technology thus produces a consensus-derived third tier of information that is higher resolution in that it is more densely modulated with quality attributes and simultaneously more global, more egalitarian, and freer flowing. The blockchain as an information technology provides high-resolution modulation regarding the quality, authenticity, and derivation of information.

Consensus data is thus data that comes with a crowd-voted confirmation of quality, a seal of approval, the vote of a populace standing behind the quality, accuracy, and truth value of the data, in its current incarnation effectuated by a seamless automated mining mechanism. The bigger questions are "What can a society do with this kind of quality of data?" or more realistically, "What can a society do with this kind of widespread mechanism for confirming data quality?" Thinking of the benefits of consensus-derived information only helps to underline that blockchain technology might be precisely the kind of core infrastructural element as well as scalable information authentication and validation mechanism necessary to scale human progress and to expand into a global and eventually beyond-planetary society. The speculative endgame vision is that the universe is information, where the vector of progress means transitioning toward higher-resolution information flows. Information may be conserved, but its density is not. Even beyond conceiving of blockchain technology as a core infrastructural element to scale the future of human progress, ultimately it might be a tool for increasing the information resolution of the universe.

Cryptocurrency Basics

Bitcoin and other altcoins are digital cash, a way of buying and selling things over the Internet. The first step is establishing a digital wallet, either via a browser-based web wallet or by downloading a desktop or smartphone wallet from Blockchain.info, Mycelium, Coinbase, Electrum, or other Bitcoin wallet providers. Your Bitcoin address as well as your public and private keys are generated automatically when you set up your wallet. Your Bitcoin address is typically an identifier of 26 to 34 alphanumeric characters, beginning with the number 1 or 3, that represents a possible destination for a Bitcoin payment—for example, `1JDQ5KSqUTBo5M3GUPx8vm9134eJRosLoH`, represented like this string of characters or as a QR code. (This example Bitcoin address is the tip jar of an informative podcast covering blockchain technology called Let's Talk Bitcoin.) Your Bitcoin address is like your email address; people with your email address can send you email; people with your public-key wallet address can send you Bitcoins.

Because Bitcoin is digital cash, your wallet does not contain the actual cash (thus the term *wallet* is a bit of a misnomer). Your wallet has your address, public and private keys, and a record of the amount of Bitcoin you control on the blockchain ledger, but not any actual cash. Your wallet should be kept as safe as any traditional wallet to protect your private keys; anyone with access to them has access to controlling or spending or transferring your Bitcoin. You should not give your private keys to any other party, or store them at an exchange (poor private-key security has been one of the contributing factors in Bitcoin-related thefts and scams).

With your address, anyone can send you Bitcoins (just as anyone can send you email with your email address). To send someone else Bitcoins, you need his address and the private-key part of your wallet where the software checks that you have control over the Bitcoins you would like to spend or transfer. To send someone Bitcoins, you scan his wallet address QR code or otherwise obtain his address characters or QR code (e.g., by email or SMS). The sender scans the QR code address of the receiver's wallet and uses the wallet application to enter additional information about the transaction, such as amount, transaction fee (usually affirming the amount prespecified by the wallet software), and any other parameters to send the receiver Bitcoins. When the sender submits the transaction, a message is broadcast from the owner of the sending address to the network that x number of coins from that address now belong to the new address. This operation is authorized by the sender's private key; if that wallet does not have the private key corresponding to those coins, the coins cannot be spent. A bona fide transaction is received nearly immediately in the receiver's wallet application, with an "unconfirmed" status. It then takes about 10 minutes for the transaction to confirm and be inscribed in the blockchain per blockchain miners. So, for large purchases such as a car or real estate, you would want to wait to see the transaction confirmed, but you wouldn't bother to do so for a coffee purchase.

Public/Private-Key Cryptography 101

When the wallet is initialized or set up for the first time, an address, public key, and private key are automatically generated. Bitcoin is based on public-key encryption, meaning that you can give out the public key freely but must keep the private key to yourself.

Bitcoin addresses are created by the software picking a random number and creating a public/private key pair (per the current standard, Elliptic Curve Digital Signature Algorithm, or ECDSA) that is mathematically related, and confirmed at the time of spending the Bitcoin. This startup operation generates the private key, but additional steps are required to generate the Bitcoin address. The Bitcoin address is not simply the public key; rather, the public key is further transformed for more effective use. It is cycled through additional encryption protocols (like SHA-256 and RIPEMD-160), a hashing operation (transforming a string of characters into a shorter fixed-length value or key that represents the original string), and administrative operations (removal of similar-looking characters, like lowercase L and uppercase I, and 0 and O; adding a checksum to the end; and adding an identifying number to the beginning of the address—for most Bitcoin addresses, this is a 1, indicating it is a public Bitcoin network address).

It is infeasible though technically possible that two different people could generate the same Bitcoin address. In such a case, both would be able to spend the coins on that particular address. The odds of this happening are so small, however, that it is almost 99.9999999999 percent impossible. A Bitcoin wallet can contain multiple addresses (one security procedure is using or generating a new address for each transaction), and one or more private keys, which are saved in the wallet file. The private keys are mathematically related to all Bitcoin addresses generated for the wallet.

In Bitcoin, a private key is usually a 256-bit number (although some wallets might use between 128 and 512 bits), which can be represented in one of several ways. Here is one example of a private key (*https://en.bitcoin.it/wiki/Private_key*) in hexadecimal format (256 bits in hexadecimal is 32 bytes, or 64 characters in the range 0–9 or A–F):

```
E9 87 3D 79 C6 D8 7D C0 FB 6A 57 78 63 33 89 F4
45 32 13 30 3D A6 1F 20 BD 67 FC 23 3A A3 32 62
```

Here is another example of a private key and its corresponding public address:

```
Private key:
79186670301299046436858412936420417076660923359050732094116068951337164773779

Public address:
1EE8rpFCSSaBmG19sLdgQLEWuDaiYVFT9J
```

Doing some sort of back calculation to derive the private key from the public key is either impossible (per the hashing operation, which is one-way only, or other techniques) or prohibitively expensive (tremendous computing power operating over a longer time than would be necessary to confirm the transaction). Only the address is needed to receive Bitcoins, whereas the public/private key pair is required to send Bitcoins.

Ledra Capital Mega Master Blockchain List

New York–based venture capital firm Ledra Capital has an ongoing attempt to brainstorm and enumerate the wide range of potential uses of blockchain technology (*http://bit.ly/blockchain_tech_uses*). Some of these categories include financial instruments; public, private, and semipublic records; physical asset keys; intangibles; and other potential applications:

I. Financial instruments, records, and models

1. Currency

2. Private equities

3. Public equities

4. Bonds

5. Derivatives (futures, forwards, swaps, options, and more complex variations)

6. Voting rights associated with any of the preceding

7. Commodities

8. Spending records

9. Trading records

10. Mortgage/loan records

11. Servicing records

12. Crowdfunding

13. Microfinance

14. Microcharity

II. Public records

    15. Land titles

    16. Vehicle registries

    17. Business license

    18. Business incorporation/dissolution records

    19. Business ownership records

    20. Regulatory records

    21. Criminal records

    22. Passports

    23. Birth certificates

    24. Death certificates

    25. Voter IDs

    26. Voting

    27. Health/safety inspections

    28. Building permits

    29. Gun permits

    30. Forensic evidence

    31. Court records

    32. Voting records

    33. Nonprofit records

    34. Government/nonprofit accounting/transparency

III. Private records

    35. Contracts

    36. Signatures

    37. Wills

    38. Trusts

    39. Escrows

    40. GPS trails (personal)

IV. Other semipublic records

    41. Degree

    42. Certifications

    43. Learning outcomes

44. Grades

45. HR records (salary, performance reviews, accomplishment)

46. Medical records

47. Accounting records

48. Business transaction records

49. Genome data

50. GPS trails (institutional)

51. Delivery records

52. Arbitration

V. Physical asset keys

53. Home/apartment keys

54. Vacation home/timeshare keys

55. Hotel room keys

56. Car keys

57. Rental car keys

58. Leased cars keys

59. Locker keys

60. Safety deposit box keys

61. Package delivery (split key between delivery firm and receiver)

62. Betting records

63. Fantasy sports records

VI. Intangibles

64. Coupons

65. Vouchers

66. Reservations (restaurants, hotels, queues, etc.)

67. Movie tickets

68. Patents

69. Copyrights

70. Trademarks

71. Software licenses

72. Videogame licenses

73. Music/movie/book licenses (DRM)

74. Domain names

75. Online identities

76. Proof of authorship/proof of prior art

VII. Other

77. Documentary records (photos, audio, video)

78. Data records (sports scores, temperature, etc.)

79. Sim cards

80. GPS network identity

81. Gun unlock codes

82. Weapons unlock codes

83. Nuclear launch codes

84. Spam control (micropayments for posting)

Endnotes and References

[1] Kayne, R. "What Is BitTorrent?" wiseGEEK, December 25, 2014. *http://www.wise geek.com/what-is-bittorrent.htm#didyouknowout.*

[2] Beal, V. "Public-key encryption." Webopedia. *http://www.webopedia.com/TERM/P/public_key_cryptography.html.*

[3] Hof, R. "Seven Months After FDA Slapdown, 23andMe Returns with New Health Report Submission." *Forbes*, June 20, 2014. *http://www.forbes.com/sites/roberthof/2014/06/20/seven-months-after-fda-slapdown-23andme-returns-with-new-health-report-submission/.*

[4] Knight, H. and B. Evangelista. "S.F., L.A. Threaten Uber, Lyft, Sidecar with Legal Action." SFGATE, September 25, 2041. *http://m.sfgate.com/bayarea/article/S-F-L-A-threaten-Uber-Lyft-Sidecar-with-5781328.php.*

[5] Although it is not strictly impossible for two files to have the same hash, the number of 64-character hashes is vastly greater than the number of files that humanity can foreseeably create. This is similar to the cryptographic standard that even though a scheme *could* be cracked, the calculation would take longer than the history of the universe.

[6] Nakamoto, S. "Bitcoin v0.1 Released." The Mail Archive, January 9, 2009. *http://www.mail-archive.com/cryptography@metzdowd.com/msg10142.html.*

[7] ———. "Bitcoin: A Peer-to-Peer Electronic Cash System." (publishing data unavailable) *https://bitcoin.org/bitcoin.pdf.*

[8] Extended from: Sigal, M. "You Say You Want a Revolution? It's Called Post-PC Computing." Radar (O'Reilly), October 24, 2011. *http://radar.oreilly.com/2011/10/post-pc-revolution.html.*

[9] Gartner. "Gartner Says the Internet of Things Installed Base Will Grow to 26 Billion Units By 2020." Gartner Press Release, December 12, 2013. *http://www.gartner.com/newsroom/id/2636073.*

[10] Omohundro, S. "Cryptocurrencies, Smart Contracts, and Artificial Intelligence." Submitted to *AI Matters* (Association for Computing Machinery), October 22, 2014. *http://steveomohundro.com/2014/10/22/cryptocurrencies-smart-contracts-and-artificial-intelligence/.*

[11] Dawson, R. "The New Layer of the Economy Enabled by M2M Payments in the Internet of Things." Trends in the Living Networks, September 16, 2014. *http://ross dawsonblog.com/weblog/archives/2014/09/new-layer-economy-enabled-m2m-payments-internet-things.html.*

[12] Petschow, K. "Cisco Visual Networking Index Predicts Annual Internet Traffic to Grow More Than 20 Percent (Reaching 1.6 Zettabytes) by 2018." Cisco Press Release, 2014. *http://newsroom.cisco.com/release/1426270.*

[13] Andreessen, M. "Why Bitcoin Matters." *The New York Times*, January 21, 2014. *http://dealbook.nytimes.com/2014/01/21/why-bitcoin-matters/?_php=true&_type=blogs&_r=0.*

[14] Lamport, L., R. Shostack, and M. Pease. (1982). "The Byzantine Generals Problem." *ACM Transactions on Programming Languages and Systems* 4, no. 3: 382–401; Philipp (handle). (2014). "Bitcoin and the Byzantine Generals Problem—A Crusade Is Needed? A Revolution?" *Financial Cryptography.* *http://financialcryptography.com/mt/archives/001522.html*; Vaurum (handle name). (2014). "A Mathematical Model for Bitcoin." (blog post). *http://blog.vaurum.com/a-mathematical-model-for-bitcoin/.*

[15] Cipher (handle name). "The Current State of Coin-Mixing Services." Depp.Dot.Web, May 25, 2014. *http://www.deepdotweb.com/2014/05/25/current-state-coin-mixing-services/.*

[16] Rizzo, P. "Coinify Raises Millions to Build Europe's Complete Bitcoin Solution." CoinDesk, September 26, 2014. *http://www.coindesk.com/coinify-raises-millions-build-europes-complete-bitcoin-solution/.*

[17] Patterson, J. "Intuit Adds BitPay to PayByCoin." Bitpay Blog, November 11, 2014. *http://blog.bitpay.com/2014/11/11/intuit-adds-bitpay-to-paybycoin.html.*

[18] Hajdarbegovic, N. "Deloitte: Media 'Distracting' from Bitcoin's Disruptive Potential." CoinDesk, June 30, 2014. *http://www.coindesk.com/deloitte-media-distracting-bitcoins-disruptive-potential/*; Anonymous. "Remittances: Over the Sea and Far Away." *The Economist*, May 19, 2012. *http://www.economist.com/node/21554740.*

[19] Levine, A.B. and A.M. Antonopoulos. "Let's Talk Bitcoin! #149: Price and Popularity." Let's Talk Bitcoin podcast, September 30, 2014. *http://letstalkbitcoin.com/blog/post/lets-talk-bitcoin-149-price-and-popularity.*

[20] Kitco News. "2013: Year of the Bitcoin." *Forbes*, December 10, 2013. *http://www.forbes.com/sites/kitconews/2013/12/10/2013-year-of-the-bitcoin/.*

[21] Gough, N. "Bitcoin Value Sinks After Chinese Exchange Move." *The New York Times*, December 18, 2013. *http://www.nytimes.com/2013/12/19/business/international/china-bitcoin-exchange-ends-renminbi-deposits.html?_r=0.*

[22] Hajdarbegovic, N. "Yuan Trades Now Make Up Over 70% of Bitcoin Volume." CoinDesk, September 5, 2014. *http://www.coindesk.com/yuan-trades-now-make-70-bitcoin-volume/.*

[23] Vigna, P. "CNET Founder Readies Bitreserve Launch in Bid to Quell Bitcoin Volatility." *The Wall Street Journal*, October 22, 2014. *http://blogs.wsj.com/moneybeat/2014/10/22/cnet-founder-readies-bitreserve-launch-in-bid-to-quell-bitcoin-volatility/*.

[24] Casey, M.J. "Dollar-Backed Digital Currency Aims to Fix Bitcoin's Volatility Dilemma." *The Wall Street Journal*, July 8, 2014. *http://blogs.wsj.com/moneybeat/2014/07/08/dollar-backed-digital-currency-aims-to-fix-bitcoins-volatility-dilemma/*.

[25] Rizzo, P. "Coinapult Launches LOCKS, Aiming to Eliminate Bitcoin Price Volatility." CoinDesk, July 29, 2014. *http://www.coindesk.com/coinapult-launches-locks-tool-eliminate-bitcoin-price-volatility/*.

[26] Yang, S. "China Bans Financial Companies from Bitcoin Transactions." *Bloomberg*, December 5, 2013. *http://www.bloomberg.com/news/2013-12-05/china-s-pboc-bans-financial-companies-from-bitcoin-transactions.html*.

[27] Orsini, L. "A Year in Bitcoin: Why We'll Still Care About the Cryptocurrency Even If It Fades." ReadWrite, December 30, 2013. *http://readwrite.com/2013/12/30/bitcoin-may-fade-2014-prediction*.

[28] Bitcoin Embassy. "Andreas M. Antonopoulos Educates Senate of Canada About Bitcoin." YouTube, October 8, 2014. *https://www.youtube.com/watch?v=xUNGFZDO8mM*.

[29] Robertson, M. and R. Bramanathan. "ATO Ruling Disappointing for Bitcoin in Australia." Lexology, August 21, 2014. *http://www.lexology.com/library/detail.aspx?g=aee6a563-ab32-442d-8575-67a940527882*.

[30] Hern, A. "Bitcoin Is Legally Property, Says US IRS. Does That Kill It as a Currency?" *The Guardian*, March 31, 2014. *http://www.theguardian.com/technology/2014/mar/31/bitcoin-legally-property-irs-currency*. See also: *http://www.irs.gov/pub/irs-drop/n-14-21.pdf*.

[31] U.S. Government Accountability Office. (2014). "Virtual Currencies: Emerging Regulatory, Law Enforcement, and Consumer Protection Challenges. GAO-14-496." Published: May 29, 2014. Publicly released: June 26, 2014. *http://www.gao.gov/products/GAO-14-496*. Pages 12–20 explain how each of the relevant federal agencies (FinCEN, banking regulators, CFPB, SEC, CFTC, and DOJ) conduct supervision of Bitcoin or virtual currency or related enforcement. *See also:* "Virtual Economies and Currencies: Additional IRS Guidance Could Reduce Tax Compliance Risks." *http://www.gao.gov/products/GAO-13-516*.

[32] Nakamoto, S. "Re: Transactions and Scripts: DUP HASH160 ... EQUALVERIFY CHECKSIG." Bitcointalk, June 17, 2010. *https://bitcointalk.org/index.php?topic=195.msg1611#msg1611*.

[33] Swanson, T. "Blockchain 2.0—Let a Thousand Chains Blossom." Let's Talk Bitcoin!, April 8, 2014. *http://letstalkbitcoin.com/blockchain-2-0-let-a-thousand-chains-blossom/*.

[34] "The Mega-Master Blockchain List," posted March 11, 2014, Ledra Capital, *http://ledracapital.com/blog/2014/3/11/bitcoin-series-24-the-mega-master-blockchain-list*.

[35] Casey, M.J. "Ripple Signs First Two U.S. Banks to Bitcoin-Inspired Payments Network." *The Wall Street Journal*, September 24, 2014. *http://blogs.wsj.com/moneybeat/2014/09/24/ripple-signs-first-two-u-s-banks-to-bitcoin-inspired-payments-network/*.

[36] Prisco, G. "Spanish Bank Bankinter Invests in Bitcoin Startup Coinffeine." CryptoCoins News, updated November 17, 2014. *https://www.cryptocoinsnews.com/spanish-bank-bankinter-invests-bitcoin-startup-coinffeine/*.

[37] Mac, R. "PayPal Takes Baby Step Toward Bitcoin, Partners with Cryptocurrency Processors." *Forbes*, September 23, 2014. *http://www.forbes.com/sites/ryanmac/2014/09/23/paypal-takes-small-step-toward-bitcoin-partners-with-cryptocurrency-processors/*.

[38] Bensinger, G. "eBay Payments Unit in Talks to Accept Bitcoin." *The Wall Street Journal*, August 14, 2014. *http://online.wsj.com/articles/ebay-payment-unit-in-talks-to-accept-bitcoin-1408052917*.

[39] Cordell, D. "Fidor Bank Partners with Kraken to Create Cryptocurrency Bank." CryptoCoins News, updated November 2, 2014. *https://www.cryptocoinsnews.com/fidor-bank-partners-kraken-create-cryptocurrency-bank/*.

[40] Casey, M.J. "TeraExchange Unveils First U.S.-Regulated Bitcoin Swaps Exchange." *The Wall Street Journal*, September 12, 2014. *http://teraexchange.com/news/2014_9_12_Tera_WSJ.pdf*.

[41] Rizzo, P. "Buttercoin Bids to Take US Business from Global Bitcoin Exchanges." CoinDesk, November 5, 2014. *http://www.coindesk.com/buttercoin-bids-take-us-business-global-bitcoin-exchanges/*. See also: *https://www.wedbush.com/sites/default/files/pdf/2014_11_14_Buttercoin_WEDBUSH.pdf*.

[42] Metz, C. "Overstock.com Assembles Coders to Create a Bitcoin-Like Stock Market." *Wired*, October 6, 2014. *http://www.wired.com/2014/10/overstock-com-assembles-coders-build-bitcoin-like-stock-market/*.

[43] Ayral, S. "Bitcoin 2.0 Crowdfunding Is Real Crowdfunding." *TechCrunch*, October 17, 2014. *http://techcrunch.com/2014/10/17/bitcoin-2-0-crowdfunding-is-real-crowdfunding/*.

[44] Hofman, A. "Bitcoin Crowdfunding Platform Swarm Announces First Decentralized Demo Day." *Bitcoin Magazine*, September 30, 2014. *http://bitcoinmagazine.com/*

16890/bitcoin-crowdfunding-platform-swarm-announces-first-decentralized-demo-day/.

[45] Casey, M.J. "BitBeat: Apple Loves Bitcoin Again, Maybe." *The Wall Street Journal*, June 30, 2014. *http://blogs.wsj.com/moneybeat/2014/06/03/bitbeat-apple-loves-bitcoin-again-maybe/.*

[46] Higgins, S. "Crowdfunding Platform Swarm Announces First Class of Startups." CoinDesk, October 17, 2014. *http://www.coindesk.com/swarm-first-class-startups-crowdfunding-platform/.*

[47] Rizzo, P. "How Koinify and Melotic Plan to Bring Order to Crypto Crowdsales." CoinDesk, November 14, 2014. *http://www.coindesk.com/koinify-melotic-plan-bring-order-crypto-crowdsales/.*

[48] Higgins, S. "Koinify Raises $1 Million for Smart Corporation Crowdfunding Platform." CoinDesk, September 17, 2014. *http://www.coindesk.com/koinify-1-million-smart-corporation-crowdfunding/.*

[49] Southurst, J. "BitFlyer Launches Japan's First Bitcoin Crowdfunding Platform." CoinDesk, September 10, 2014. *http://www.coindesk.com/bitflyer-launches-japans-first-bitcoin-crowdfunding-platform/.*

[50] Swan, M. "Singularity University Live Prediction Markets Simulation and Big Data Quantitative Indicators." Slideshare, updated July 11, 2014. *http://www.slideshare.net/lablogga/singularity-university-live-prediction-markets-simulation-big-data-indicators.*

[51] No relation to this author!

[52] Swan, M. "Identity Authentication and Security Access 2.0." Broader Perspective blog, April 7, 2013. *http://futurememes.blogspot.com/2013/04/identity-authentication-and-security.html.*

[53] Szabo, N. "Formalizing and Securing Relationships on Public Networks." First Monday, September 1, 1997. *http://firstmonday.org/ojs/index.php/fm/article/view/548/469* as expounded by Hearn, M. (2014). Bitcoin Wiki. *https://en.bitcoin.it/wiki/Smart_Property.*

[54] Swanson, T. *Great Chain of Numbers: A Guide to Smart Contracts, Smart Property, and Trustless Asset Management.*

[55] Hajdarbegovic, N. "Coinprism Releases Colored Coins Android App for Mobile Asset Transfer." CoinDesk, October 20, 2014. *http://www.coindesk.com/coinprism-mobile-wallet-colored-coins/.*

[56] De Filippi, P. "Primavera De Filippi on Ethereum: Freenet or Skynet? The Berkman Center for Internet and Society at Harvard University." YouTube, April 15, 2014. *https://www.youtube.com/watch?v=slhuidzccpI.*

[57] Ibid.

[58] GSB Daily Blog. "Bitcoinomics, Chap. 11: The Future of Money and Property or the Gospel Of Layers." GoldSilverBitcoin, August 18, 2013. *https://www.goldsilverbit coin.com/future-of-money-bitcoinomic/.*

[59] Carney, M. Growing Pains: Stellar Stumbles Briefly Amid Its Launch of a New Crypto-Currency Platform." PandoDaily, August 5, 2014. *http://pando.com/ 2014/08/05/growing-pains-stellar-stumbles-briefly-amid-its-launch-of-a-new-crypto- currency-platform/.*

[60] Benet, J. "IPFS—Content Addressed, Versioned, P2P File System (DRAFT 3)." Accessed 2014. (no publishing or posting data available) *http://static.benet.ai/t/ ipfs.pdf.*

[61] Atkin, A. "TrustDavis on Ethereum." Slideshare, June 19, 2014. *http://www.slide share.net/aatkin1971/trustdavis-on-ethereum.*

[62] Galt, J. "Crypto Swartz Will Get You Paid for Your Great Content." The CoinFront, June 23, 2014. *http://thecoinfront.com/crypto-swartz-will-get-you-paid-for-your-great- content/.*

[63] Prisco, G. "Counterparty Recreates Ethereum on Bitcoin." CryptoCoins News, updated November 12, 2014. *https://www.cryptocoinsnews.com/counterparty- recreates-ethereum-bitcoin/. See also:* "Counterparty Recreates Ethereum's Smart Contract Platform on Bitcoin." Counterparty Press Release. *http://counterparty.io/news/ counterparty-recreates-ethereums-smart-contract-platform-on-bitcoin/.*

[64] Swan, M. "Counterparty/Ethereum: Why Bitcoin Topped $450 Today (Was Under $350 Last Week)." Broader Perspective blog, November 12, 2014. *http://future memes.blogspot.com/2014/11/counterpartyethereum-why-bitcoin-topped.html.*

[65] "DEV PLAN," Ethereum, accessed 2014, *https://www.ethereum.org/pdfs/Ethereum- Dev-Plan-preview.pdf.*

[66] Finley, K. "Out in the Open: An NSA-Proof Twitter, Built with Code from Bitcoin and BitTorrent." *Wired*, January 13, 2014. *http://www.wired.com/2014/01/twister/.*

[67] Johnston, D. et al. "The General Theory of Decentralized Applications, DApps." GitHub, June 9, 2014. *https://github.com/DavidJohnstonCEO/DecentralizedApplica tions.*

[68] Babbitt, D. "Crypto-Economic Design: A Proposed Agent-Based Modeling Effort." SwarmFest 2014: 18th Annual Meeting on Agent-Based Modeling & Simulation. University of Notre Dame, Notre Dame, IN. June 29 through July 1, 2014. *http:// www3.nd.edu/~swarm06/SwarmFest2014/Crypto-economicDesignBabbit.pdf.*

[69] Butarin, V. "Bootstrapping a Decentralized Autonomous Corporation: Part I." *Bit- coin Magazine*, September 19, 2013. *http://bitcoinmagazine.com/7050/bootstrapping-a-*

decentralized-autonomous-corporation-part-i/; Bontje, J. "Ethereum—Decentralized Autonomous Organizations." Slideshare, April 9, 2014. *http://www.slideshare.net/mids106/ethereum-decentralized-autonomous-organizations*; Ethereum (EtherCasts). "Egalitarian DAO Contract Explained." YouTube, April 3, 2014. *https://www.youtube.com/watch?v=Q_gxDytSvuY*.

[70] Spaven, E. "Cloud Storage Startup Storj Raises 910 BTC in Crowdsale." CoinDesk, August 22, 2014. *http://www.coindesk.com/cloud-storage-startup-storj-raises-910-btc-crowdsale/*.

[71] Marckx, C. "Storj: Next-Generation Cloud Storage Through the Blockchain." CryptoCoins News, updated April 11, 2014. *https://www.cryptocoinsnews.com/storj-next-generation-cloud-storage-through-the-blockchain/*.

[72] Levine, A.B. "Application Specific, Autonomous, Self-Bootstrapping Consensus Platforms." Bitsharestalk forum, January 1, 2014. *https://bitsharestalk.org/index.php?topic=1854.0*.

[73] Swan, M. "Automatic Markets." Broader Perspective blog, August 23, 2009. *http://futurememes.blogspot.com/2009/08/automatic-markets.html*.

[74] Hearn, M. "Future of Money (and Everything Else)." Edinburgh Turing Festival. YouTube, August 23, 2013. *https://www.youtube.com/watch?v=Pu4PAMFPo5Y*.

[75] Moshinsky, B. et al. "WikiLeaks Finds Snowden Cash Bump Elusive." *Bloomberg Businessweek*, July 11, 2013. *http://www.businessweek.com/articles/2013-07-11/wikileaks-finds-snowden-cash-bump-elusive*.

[76] Gilson, D. "What Are Namecoins and .bit Domains?" CoinDesk, June 18, 2013. *http://www.coindesk.com/what-are-namecoins-and-bit-domains/*.

[77] ———. "Developers Attempt to Resurrect Namecoin After Fundamental Flaw Discovered." CoinDesk, October 28, 2013. *http://www.coindesk.com/namecoin-flaw-patch-needed/*.

[78] Wong, J.I. "Trend Micro Report Finds Criminals Unlikely to Abuse Namecoin." CoinDesk, July 18, 2014. *http://www.coindesk.com/trend-micro-report-finds-criminals-unlikely-abuse-namecoin/*.

[79] McArdle, R. and D. Sancho. "Bitcoin Domains: A Trend Micro Research Paper." Trend Micro, accessed 2013 (publishing data unavailable). *http://www.trendmicro.com.au/cloud-content/us/pdfs/security-intelligence/white-papers/wp-bitcoin-domains.pdf*.

[80] Michael J. "Dotp2p Demo Video." YouTube, July 10, 2014. *https://www.youtube.com/watch?feature=youtu.be&v=qeweF05tT50&app=desktop*.

[81] BTC Geek. "Bitshares DNS KeyID Starts Trading." BTC Geek blog, accessed 2014 (publishing data unavailable). *http://btcgeek.com/bitshares-dns-keyid-starts-trading/*.

82 Twitter. "Tweets Still Must Flow." Twitter Blog, January 26, 2012. *https://blog.twitter.com/2012/tweets-still-must-flow.*

83 Dollentas, N. "Exclusive Q&A with Joseph Fiscella: Florincoin and Decentralized Applications." Bitoinist.net, June 22, 2014. *http://bitcoinist.net/exclusive-qa-with-joseph-fiscella-florincoin-and-decentralized-applications/.*

84 Chaffin, B. "The NSA Can Listen to Skype Calls (Thanks to Microsoft)." *The Mac Observer,* July 11, 2013. *http://www.macobserver.com/tmo/article/the-nsa-can-listen-to-skype-calls-thanks-to-microsoft*; Goodin, D. Encrypted or Not, Skype Communications Prove 'Vital' to NSA Surveillance." Ars Technica, May 13, 2014. *http://arstechnica.com/security/2014/05/encrypted-or-not-skype-communications-prove-vital-to-nsa-surveillance/.*

85 Brin, D. *The Transparent Society: Will Technology Force Us to Choose Between Privacy and Freedom?* Cambridge, MA: Perseus Books Group, 1999.

86 Chaffin, B. "The NSA Can Listen to Skype Calls (Thanks to Microsoft)." *The Mac Observer,* July 11, 2013. *http://www.macobserver.com/tmo/article/the-nsa-can-listen-to-skype-calls-thanks-to-microsoft.*

87 Dourado, E. "Can Namecoin Obsolete ICANN (and More)?" The Ümlaut, February 5, 2014. *http://theumlaut.com/2014/02/05/namecoin-icann/.*

88 Rizzo, P. "How OneName Makes Bitcoin Payments as Simple as Facebook Sharing." CoinDesk, March 27, 2014. *http://www.coindesk.com/onename-makes-bitcoin-payments-simple-facebook-sharing/.*

89 Higgins, S. "Authentication Protocol BitID Lets Users 'Connect with Bitcoin.'" Coin-Desk, May 7, 2014. *http://www.coindesk.com/authentication-protocol-bitid-lets-users-connect-bitcoin/.*

90 Rohan, M. "Multi-Factor Authentication Market Worth $10.75 Billion by 2020." Markets and Markets, accessed 2014 (publishing data unavailable). *htt (http://www.marketsandmarkets.com/PressReleases/multi-factor-authentication.asp)p://www.marketsandmarkets.com/PressReleases/multi-factor-authentication.asp (http://www.marketsandmarkets.com/PressReleases/multi-factor-authentication.asp).*

91 Antonopoulos, A.M. "Bitcoin Neutrality." Bitcoin 2013 Conference, May 18, 2013, San Jose, CA. YouTube, June 10, 2013. *https://www.youtube.com/watch?v=BT8FXQN-9-A.*

92 Senbonzakura (handle name). "Islamic Bank of Bitcoin." Bitcoin Forum, June 24, 2011. *https://bitcointalk.org/index.php?topic=21732.0.*

93 Chaia, A. et al. "Half the World Is Unbanked." McKinsey & Co, March 2009. *http://mckinseyonsociety.com/half-the-world-is-unbanked/.*

[94] "2013 FDIC National Survey of Unbanked and Underbanked Households," U.S. Federal Deposit Insurance Corporation, updated October 28, 2014, *https:// www.fdic.gov/householdsurvey/*.

[95] Mims, C. "M-Pesa: 31% of Kenya's GDP Is Spent Through Mobile Phones." Quartz, February 27, 2013. *http://qz.com/57504/31-of-kenyas-gdp-is-spent-through-mobile-phones/*.

[96] Cawrey, D. "37Coins Plans Worldwide Bitcoin Access with SMS-Based Wallet." CoinDesk, May 20, 2014. *http://www.coindesk.com/37coins-plans-worldwide-bitcoin-access-sms-based-wallet/*.

[97] Rizzo, P. "How Kipochi Is Taking Bitcoin into Africa." CoinDesk, April 25, 2014. *http://www.coindesk.com/kipochi-taking-bitcoin-africa/*.

[98] It is not impossible that two files could produce the same hash, but the chance is one in trillions of trillions or more.

[99] Cawrey, D. "How Bitcoin's Technology Could Revolutionize Intellectual Property Rights." CoinDesk, May 8, 2014. *http://www.coindesk.com/how-block-chain-technology-is-working-to-transform-intellectual-property/*.

[100] Kirk, J. "Could the Bitcoin Network Be Used as an Ultrasecure Notary Service?" *Computerworld*, May 23, 2013. *http://www.computerworld.com/article/2498077/desktop-apps/could-the-bitcoin-network-be-used-as-an-ultrasecure-notary-service-.html*.

[101] Morgan, P. "Using Blockchain Technology to Prove Existence of a Document." Empowered Law, accessed 2014. *http://empoweredlaw.wordpress.com/2014/03/11/using-blockchain-technology-to-prove-existence-of-a-document/*.

[102] Sirer, EG. "Introducing Virtual Notary." Hacking, Distributed, June 20, 2013. *hackingdistributed.com/2013/06/20/virtual-notary-intro/*.

[103] Goss, L. "The High School Startup Using Blockchain Technology." BitScan, August 27, 2014. *https://bitscan.com/articles/the-high-school-startup-using-blockchain-technology*.

[104] Cawrey, D. "How Monegraph Uses the Block Chain to Verify Digital Assets." CoinDesk, May 15, 2014. *http://www.coindesk.com/monegraph-uses-block-chain-verify-digital-assets/*.

[105] Snow, P. "Notary Chains" (white paper). *https://github.com/NotaryChains/*.

[106] Stephenson, N. *Snow Crash*. New York: Spectra, 1992. *See also: http://every thing2.com/title/Franchulate*.

[107] Swan, M. "Illiberty in Biohacking, Personal Data Rights, Neuro-diversity, and the Automation Economy." Broader Perspective blog, March 2, 2014. *http://future memes.blogspot.fr/2014/03/illiberty-in-biohacking-personal-data.html*.

[108] Prisco, G. "Bitcoin Governance 2.0: Let's Block-chain Them." CryptoCoins News, updated October 13, 2014. *https://www.cryptocoinsnews.com/bitcoin-governance-2-0-lets-block-chain/*.

[109] Hofman, A. "Couple to Get Married on the Bitcoin Blockchain at Disney Bitcoin Conference." *Bitcoin Magazine*, September 23, 2014. *http://bitcoinmagazine.com/16771/couple-get-married-bitcoin-blockchain-disney-bitcoin-conference/*.

[110] Marty, B. "Couple Make History with World's First Bitcoin Wedding." *PanAm Post*, October 7, 2014. *http://panampost.com/belen-marty/2014/10/07/couple-make-history-with-worlds-first-bitcoin-wedding/*.

[111] Ploshay, E. "A Word from Jeffrey Tucker: Bitcoin Is Not a Monetary System." *Bitcoin Magazine*, January 3, 2014. *http://bitcoinmagazine.com/9299/word-jeffrey-tucker-bitcoin-monetary-system/*.

[112] McMillan, R. "Hacker Dreams Up Crypto Passport Using the Tech Behind Bitcoin." *Wired*, October 30, 2014. *http://www.wired.com/2014/10/world_passport/*; Ellis, C. "World Citizenship Project Features in Wired Magazine." Blog post, November 1, 2014. *http://chrisellis.me/world-citizenship-project-features-in-wired-magazine/*.

[113] De Soto, H. *The Mystery of Capital: Why Capitalism Triumphs in the West and Fails Everywhere Else*. New York: Basic Books, 2003.

[114] Swan, M. "Crowdsourced Health Research Studies: An Important Emerging Complement to Clinical Trials in the Public Health Research Ecosystem." *J Med Internet Res* 14, no. 2 (2012): e46.

[115] Mishra, P. "Inside India's Aadhar, the World's Biggest Biometrics Database." TechCrunch, December 6, 2013. *http://techcrunch.com/2013/12/06/inside-indias-aadhar-the-worlds-biggest-biometrics-database/*.

[116] Deitz, J. "Decentralized Governance Whitepaper." Quora, May 21, 2014. *http://distributed-autonomous-society.quora.com/Decentralized-Governance-Whitepaper*.

[117] Ramos, J. "Liquid Democracy: The App That Turns Everyone into a Politician." Shareable, January 20, 2014. *http://www.shareable.net/blog/liquid-democracy-the-app-that-turns-everyone-into-a-politician*.

[118] Buchanan, A.E. *Deciding for Others: The Ethics of Surrogate Decision Making (Studies in Philosophy and Health Policy)*. Cambridge: Cambridge University Press, 1990.

[119] Carroll, L. *The Principles of Parliamentary Representation*. London: Harrison and Sons, 1884. *https://archive.org/details/ThePrinciplesOfParliamentaryRepresentation*;

Black, D. "The Central Argument in Lewis Carroll's *The Principles of Parliamentary Representation*." *Papers on Non-market Decision Making* 3, no 1 (1967): 1–17.

[120] Chaum, D. "Random-Sample Elections: Far Lower Cost, Better Quality and More Democratic." Accessed 2012 (publishing data unavailable). *www.rs-elections.com/Random-Sample%20Elections.pdf*.

[121] Davis, J. "How Selecting Voters Randomly Can Lead to Better Elections." *Wired*, May 16, 2012. www.wired.com/2012/05/st_essay_voting/.

[122] Hanson, R. "Futarchy: Vote Values, but Bet Beliefs." Accessed 2013 (publishing data unavailable). *http://hanson.gmu.edu/futarchy2013.pdf*.

[123] Buterin, V. "An Introduction to Futarchy [as Applied with Blockchain Technology]." Ethereum blog, August 21, 2014. *https://blog.ethereum.org/2014/08/21/introduction-futarchy/*.

[124] Cruz, K. "The Truth Behind Truthcoin." *Bitcoin Magazine*, September 25, 2014. *http://bitcoinmagazine.com/16748/truth-behind-truthcoin/*.

[125] Wagner, A. "Putting the Blockchain to Work For Science!" *Bitcoin Magazine*, May 22, 2014. *http://bitcoinmagazine.com/13187/putting-the-blockchain-to-work-for-science-gridcoin/*.

[126] Buterin, V. "Primecoin: The Cryptocurrency Whose Mining Is Actually Useful." *Bitcoin Magazine*, July 8, 2013. *http://bitcoinmagazine.com/5635/primecoin-the-cryptocurrency-whose-mining-is-actually-useful/*.

[127] Myers, D.S., A.L. Bazinet, and M.P. Cummings. "Expanding the Reach of Grid Computing: Combining Globus-and BOINC-Based Systems." Center for Bioinformatics and Computational Biology, Institute for Advanced Computer Studies, University of Maryland, February 6, 2007 (Draft). *http://lattice.umiacs.umd.edu/latticefiles/publications/lattice/myers_bazinet_cummings.pdf*.

[128] Clenfield, J. and P. Alpeyev. "The Other Bitcoin Power Struggle." *Bloomberg Businessweek*, April 24, 2014. *http://www.businessweek.com/articles/2014-04-24/bitcoin-miners-seek-cheap-electricity-to-eke-out-a-profit*.

[129] Gimein, M. "Virtual Bitcoin Mining Is a Real-World Environmental Disaster." *Bloomberg*, April 12, 2013. *http://www.bloomberg.com/news/2013-04-12/virtual-bitcoin-mining-is-a-real-world-environmental-disaster.html*.

[130] Worstall, T. "Fascinating Number: Bitcoin Mining Uses $15 Million's Worth of Electricity Every Day." *Forbes*, December 3, 2013. *http://www.forbes.com/sites/timworstall/2013/12/03/fascinating-number-bitcoin-mining-uses-15-millions-worth-of-electricity-every-day/*.

[131] Tapscott, D. and A.D. Williams. *Wikinomics: How Mass Collaboration Changes Everything*. New York: Penguin Group, 2008.

[132] Anonymous. "EteRNA." *Scientific American*, (publishing data unavailable). *http://www.scientificamerican.com/citizen-science/eterna/*.

[133] Vigna, P. and M.J. Casey. "BitBeat: Could Bitcoin Help Fight the Ebola Crisis?" *The Wall Street Journal*, October 8, 2014. *http://blogs.wsj.com/moneybeat/2014/10/08/bitbeat-could-bitcoin-help-fight-the-ebola-crisis/*.

[134] Cawrey, D. "37Coins Plans Worldwide Bitcoin Access with SMS-Based Wallet." CoinDesk, May 20, 2014. *http://www.coindesk.com/37coins-plans-worldwide-bitcoin-access-sms-based-wallet/*.

[135] Rizzo, P. "How Kipochi Is Taking Bitcoin into Africa." CoinDesk, April 25, 2014. *http://www.coindesk.com/kipochi-taking-bitcoin-africa/*.

[136] Mims, C. "M-Pesa: 31% of Kenya's GDP Is Spent Through Mobile Phones." Quartz, February 27, 2013. *http://qz.com/57504/31-of-kenyas-gdp-is-spent-through-mobile-phones/*.

[137] Buterin, V. "Sean's Outpost Announces Satoshi Forest, Nine-Acre Sanctuary for the Homeless." *Bitcoin Magazine*, September 9, 2013. *http://bitcoinmagazine.com/6939/seans-outpost-announces-satoshi-forest/*.

[138] Green, R. and N.A. Farahany. "Regulation: The FDA Is Overcautious on Consumer Genomics." *Nature*, January 15, 2014. *http://www.nature.com/news/regulation-the-fda-is-overcautious-on-consumer-genomics-1.14527*.

[139] Wright, C. et al. "People Have a Right to Access Their Own Genetic Information." Genomes Unzipped: Personal Public Genomes, November 3, 2011. *http://genomesunzipped.org/2011/03/people-have-a-right-to-access-their-own-genetic-information.php*.

[140] Green, R.C. et al. "Disclosure of APOE Genotype for Risk of Alzheimer's Disease." *New England Journal of Medicine* 361 (July 16, 2009):245–54. *http://www.nejm.org/doi/full/10.1056/NEJMoa0809578* and discussed in further detail at *http://www.genomes2people.org/director/*.

[141] Regalado, A. "The FDA Ordered 23andMe to Stop Selling Its Health Tests. But for the Intrepid, Genome Knowledge Is Still Available." *MIT Technology Review*, October 19, 2014. *http://www.technologyreview.com/featuredstory/531461/how-a-wiki-is-keeping-direct-to-consumer-genetics-alive/*.

[142] DeCODEme. "Sales of Genetic Scans Direct to Consumer Through deCODEme Have Been Discontinued! Existing Customers Can Access Their Results Here Until January 1st 2015." *http://en.wikipedia.org/wiki/DeCODE_genetics*.

[143] Castillo, M. "23andMe to Only Provide Ancestry, Raw Genetics Data During FDA Review." CBS News, December 6, 2013. *http://www.cbsnews.com/news/23andme-to-still-provide-ancestry-raw-genetics-data-during-fda-review/*.

[144] Swan, M. "Health 2050: The Realization of Personalized Medicine Through Crowdsourcing, the Quantified Self, and the Participatory Biocitizen." *J Pers Med* 2, no. 3 (2012): 93–118.

[145] ———. "Multigenic Condition Risk Assessment in Direct-to-Consumer Genomic Services. *Genet Med* 12, no. 5 (2010): 279–88; Kido, T. et al. "Systematic Evaluation of Personal Genome Services for Japanese Individuals." *Nature: Journal of Human Genetics* 58 (2013):734–41.

[146] Tamblyn, T. "Backup Your DNA Using Bitcoins." Huffington Post UK, October 30, 2014. *http://www.huffingtonpost.co.uk/2014/10/30/genecoin-genome-backup-bitcoin_n_6076366.html.*

[147] Grens, K. "Cloud-Based Genomics." *The Scientist*, October 28, 2013. *http://www.the-scientist.com/?articles.view/articleNo/38044/title/Cloud-Based-Genomics/.*

[148] Jiang, K. "University of Chicago to Establish Genomic Data Commons." University of Chicago News, December 2, 2014. *http://news.uchicago.edu/article/2014/12/02/university-chicago-establish-genomic-data-commons.*

[149] Swan, M. "Blockchain Health—Remunerative Health Data Commons & Health-Coin RFPs." Broader Perspective blog, September 28, 2014. *http://futurememes.blogspot.com/2014/09/blockchain-health-remunerative-health.html.*

[150] HL7 Standards. "20 Questions for Health IT #5: Bitcoin & Blockchain Technology." HL7 Standards, September 8, 2014. *http://www.hl7standards.com/blog/2014/09/08/20hit-5/.*

[151] Zimmerman, J. "DNA Block Chain Project Boosts Research, Preserves Patient Anonymity." CoinDesk, June 27, 2014. *http://www.coindesk.com/israels-dna-bits-moves-beyond-currency-with-genes-blockchain/.*

[152] Swan, M. "Quantified Self Ideology: Personal Data Becomes Big Data." Slideshare, February 6, 2014. *http://www.slideshare.net/lablogga/quantified-self-ideology-personal-data-becomes-big-data.*

[153] Levine, A.B. "Let's Talk Bitcoin! #158: Ebola and the Body Blockchain with Kevin J. McKernan." Let's Talk Bitcoin podcast, November 1, 2014. *http://letstalkbitcoin.com/blog/post/lets-talk-bitcoin-158-ebola-and-the-body-blockchain.*

[154] McKernan, K. "Niemann-Pick Type C & Ebolavirus: Bitcoin Community Comes Together to Advocate and Fund Open Source Ebolavirus Research." Medicinal Genomics, accessed 2014 (publishing data unavailable). *http://www.medicinalgenomics.com/niemann-pick-type-c-and-ebola/.*

[155] Anonymous. "The Evolving Genetics of HIV: Can Genes Stop HIV?" The Tech Museum of Innovation, (publishing data unavailable). *http://genetics.thetech.org/original_news/news13.*

[156] Anonymous. "Unreliable Research. Trouble at the Lab." *The Economist*, October 17, 2013 (paywall restricted). *http://www.economist.com/news/briefing/21588057-scientists-think-science-self-correcting-alarming-degree-it-not-trouble.*

[157] Schmidt, M. and H. Lipson. "Distilling Free-Form Natural Laws from Experimental Data." *Science* 324, no. 5923 (2009): 81–5. *http://creativemachines.cornell.edu/sites/default/files/Science09_Schmidt.pdf*; Keim, B. "Computer Program Self-Discovers Laws of Physics." *Wired*, April 2, 2009. *http://www.wired.com/2009/04/newtonai/.*

[158] Muggleton, S. "Developing Robust Synthetic Biology Designs Using a Microfluidic Robot Scientist. Advances in Artificial Intelligence—SBIA 2008." Lecture notes in *Computer Science* 5249 (2008):4. *http://link.springer.com/chapter/10.1007/978-3-540-88190-2_3.*

[159] Waltz, D. and BG Buchanan. "Automating Science." *Science* 324, no. 5923 (2009): 43–4. *http://www.sciencemag.org/content/324/5923/43.*

[160] Higgins, S. "Sidechains White Paper Imagines New Future for Digital Currency Development." Coindesk, October 23, 2014. *http://www.coindesk.com/sidechains-white-paper-ecosystem-reboot/*; Back, A. et al. "Enabling Blockchain Innovations with Pegged Sidechains." Accessed 2014 (publishing data unavailable). *http://www.block stream.com/sidechains.pdf.*

[161] daCosta, F. *Rethinking the Internet of Things: A Scalable Approach to Connecting Everything.* New York: Apress, 2013.

[162] Deleuze, G. *Cinema 2: The Time-Image.* Minneapolis: University of Minnesota Press, 1989.

[163] Heidegger, M. *Being and Time.* New York: Harper Perennial Modern Classics, 1927.

[164] Crackerhead (handle name). "Mining LTBCoin." BitcoinTalk.org forum, July 27, 2014. *https://bitcointalk.org/index.php?topic=712944.0.*

[165] von Hayek, F.A. *Denationalization of Money: An Analysis of the Theory and Practice of Concurrent Currencies.* London: Institute of Economic Affairs, 1977.

[166] ———. "The 'Paradox' of Saving." *Economica*, no. 32 (1931).

[167] Blumen, R. "Hayek on the Paradox of Saving." Ludwig von Mises Institute, January 9, 2008. *http://mises.org/daily/2804.*

[168] Ferrara, P. "Rethinking Money: The Rise Of Hayek's Private Competing Currencies." *Forbes*, March 1, 2013. *http://www.forbes.com/sites/peterferrara/2013/03/01/rethinking-money-the-rise-of-hayeks-private-competing-currencies/.*

[169] Wong, J.I. "MIT Undergrads Can Now Claim Their Free $100 in Bitcoin." Coin-Desk, October 29, 2014. *http://www.coindesk.com/mit-undergrads-can-now-claim-free-100-bitcoin/*.

[170] Rizzo, P. "70,000 Caribbean Island Residents to Receive Bitcoin in 2015." Coin-Desk, August 28, 2014. *http://www.coindesk.com/70000-caribbean-island-residents-receive-bitcoin-2015/*.

[171] Cawrey, D. "Auroracoin Airdrop: Will Iceland Embrace a National Digital Currency?" CoinDesk, March 24, 2014. *http://www.coindesk.com/auroracoin-airdrop-iceland-embrace-national-digital-currency/*.

[172] Khaosan, V. "Ecuador: The First Nation to Create Its Own Digital Currency." CryptoCoins News, updated August 1, 2014. *https://www.cryptocoinsnews.com/ecuador-first-nation-create-digital-currency/*.

[173] Hamill, J. "The Battle of Little Bitcoin: Native American Tribe Launches Its Own Cryptocurrency." *Forbes*, February 27, 2014. *http://www.forbes.com/sites/jasperhamill/2014/02/27/the-battle-of-little-bitcoin-native-american-tribe-launches-its-own-cryptocurrency/*.

[174] Lietaerm, B. and J. Dunne. *Rethinking Money: How New Currencies Turn Scarcity into Prosperity* London: Berrett-Koehler Publishers, 2013.

[175] Swan, M. "Social Economic Networks and the New Intangibles." Broader Perspective blog, August 15, 2010. *http://futurememes.blogspot.com/2010/08/social-economic-networks-and-new.html*.

[176] ———. "New Banks, New Currencies, and New Markets in a Multicurrency World: Roadmap for a Post-Scarcity Economy by 2050." Create Futures IberoAmérica, Enthusiasmo Cultural, São Paolo Brazil, October 14, 2009.

[177] ———. "Connected World Wearables Free Cognitive Surplus." Broader Perspective blog, October 26, 2014. *http://futurememes.blogspot.com/2014/10/connected-world-frees-cognitive-surplus.html*.

[178] Lee, T.B. "Bitcoin Needs to Scale by a Factor of 1000 to Compete with Visa. Here's How to Do It." *The Washington Post*, November 12, 2013. *http://www.washingtonpost.com/blogs/the-switch/wp/2013/11/12/bitcoin-needs-to-scale-by-a-factor-of-1000-to-compete-with-visa-heres-how-to-do-it/*.

[179] Spaven, E. "The 12 Best Answers from Gavin Andresen's Reddit AMA." CoinDesk, October 21, 2014. *http://www.coindesk.com/12-answers-gavin-andresen-reddit-ama/*.

[180] Prashar, V. "What Is Bitcoin 51% Attack, Should I Be Worried?" BTCpedia, April 21, 2013. *http://www.btcpedia.com/bitcoin-51-attack/*.

[181] Rizzo, P. "Ghash.io: We Will Never Launch a 51% Attack Against Bitcoin." Coin-Desk, June 16, 2014. *http://www.coindesk.com/ghash-io-never-launch-51-attack/*.

[182] Courtois, N. "How to Upgrade the Bitcoin Elliptic Curve." Financial Cryptography, Bitcoin, Crypto Currencies blog, November 16, 2014. *http://blog.bettercrypto.com/?p=1008.*

[183] Ibid.

[184] Kwon, J. "Tendermint: Consensus Without Mining" Accessed 2014 (white paper). *http://tendermint.com/docs/tendermint.pdf.*

[185] ———. "Tendermint Consensus Proposal." Bitcoin forum, November 20, 2014. *https://bitcointalk.org/index.php?topic=866460.0.* See also tendermint.com/posts/security-of-cryptocurrency-protocols/.

[186] Anonymous. "The Troubling Holes in MtGox's Account of How It Lost $600 Million in Bitcoins." *MIT Technology Review*, April 4, 2014. *http://www.technologyreview.com/view/526161/the-troubling-holes-in-mtgoxs-account-of-how-it-lost-600-million-in-bitcoins/.*

[187] Collier, K. "Moolah CEO Accused of Disappearing with $1.4 Million in Bitcoin." Daily Dot, October 21, 2014. *http://www.dailydot.com/politics/moolah-dogecoin-alex-green-ryan-kennedy-ryan-gentle-millions-missing-mintpal/.*

[188] Pick, L. "Nearly $2 Million Worth of Vericoin Stolen from MintPal, Hard Fork Implemented." Digital Currency Magnates, July 15, 2014. *http://dcmagnates.com/nearly-2-million-worth-of-vericoin-stolen-from-mintpal-hard-fork-considered/.*

[189] Greenberg, A. "Hacker Hijacks Storage Devices, Mines $620,000 in Dogecoin." *Wired*, June 17, 2014. *http://www.wired.com/2014/06/hacker-hijacks-storage-devices-mines-620000-in-dogecoin/.*

[190] Swan, M. "Scaling Crowdsourced Health Studies: The Emergence of a New Form of Contract Research Organization." *Pers Med.* 9, no. 2 (2012): 223–34.

[191] Reitman, R. "Beware the BitLicense: New York's Virtual Currency Regulations Invade Privacy and Hamper Innovation." Electronic Frontier Foundation, October 15, 2014. *https://www.eff.org/deeplinks/2014/10/beware-bitlicense-new-yorks-virtual-currency-regulations-invade-privacy-and-hamper.*

[192] Santori, M. "What New York's Proposed Regulations Mean for Bitcoin Businesses." CoinDesk, July 18, 2014. *http://www.coindesk.com/new-yorks-proposed-regulations-mean-bitcoin-businesses/.*

[193] Cowen, T. *Average Is Over: Powering America Beyond the Age of the Great Stagnation.* New York: Dutton Publishing, 2013.

[194] Antonopoulos, A.M. *Mastering Bitcoin: Unlocking Digital Crypto-Currencies.* Sebastopol, CA: O'Reilly Media, 2014.

[195] Bostrom, N. *Superintelligence: Paths, Dangers, Strategies.* Oxford, UK: Oxford University Press, 2014.

[196] Swan, M. "Blockchain-Enforced Friendly AI." Crypto Money Expo, December 5, 2014. *http://cryptomoneyexpo.com/expos/inv2/#schedule* and *http://youtu.be/ qdGoRep5iT0/.*

Index

franculates, 46
freedom of speech, 34, 35
    (see also decentralized DNS system)
Freicoin, 78
fundraising (see crowdfunding)
futarchy, 53-54

G

GBIcoin, 78
GBIs (Guaranteed Basic Income initiatives), 78
Gems, 19, 23
Genecoin, 59
Genomecoin, 60
Genomic Data Commons, 60
genomic sequencing, 59-61
GenomicResearchcoin, 61
genomics, consumer, 58-61
Git, 20
GitHub, 65, 77
global public health, 57
GoCoin, 11
GoToLunchcoin, 72
governance, 46-54
    decentralized services, 47-50
    dispute resolution, 50
    futarchy, 53-54
    Liquid Democracy system, 51-52
    personalized governance services, 46
    random-sample elections, 52
    societal maturity impact of blockchain gov-
        ernance, 54
government regulation, 7, 89-90
Gridcoin, 55-56

H

hashing, 39-42, 45, 86
Hayek, Friedrich, 73, 78, 93, 94
health, 61-63
    as demurrage currency, 80
    doctor vendor RFP services, 63
    health notary services, 63
    health research commons , 62
    health spending, 61
    healthcare decision making and advocacy,
        52
    personal health record storage, 61
    virus bank and seed vault backup, 63
Healthcoin, 61, 78

I

identity authentication, 4, 10, 14, 15, 19, 36-39,
    42, 48, 52, 64, 90
Indiegogo, 12, 24
industry scandals, 88
infrastructure needs and issues, 85
inheritance gifts, 17
intellectual property, 43
    (see also digital art)
Internet administration, 33
Internet Archive, 21, 46
Internet censorship prevention (see Decentral-
    ized DNS system)
Intuit Quickbooks, 4
IP protection, 40
IPFS project, 20

J

Johnston, David, 31
Journalcoin, 66
Judobaby, 13
justice applications
    for censorship-resistant organizational
        models, 32-33
    digital art, 39-46
        (see also digital art, blockchain attesta-
            tion services)
    digital identity verification, 10, 14, 19,
        36-39, 42, 49, 52, 64, 90
    freedom of speech/anti-censorship, 35
    governance, 46-54
        (see also governance)
    Namecoin, 33-36, 43
        (see also decentralized DNS)

K

Kickstarter, 12, 56
Kipochi, 38, 57, 64
Koinify, 13, 23
Kraken, 12

L

latency, 18, 84, 86, 89
LaZooz, 23, 74, 80
Learncoin, 64
learning and literacy, 63-65
learning contract exchanges, 65
Ledra Capital, 10, 103

About the Author

Melanie Swan is the Founder of the Institute for Blockchain Studies and a Contemporary Philosophy MA candidate at Kingston University London and Université Paris VIII. She has a traditional markets background with an MBA in Finance from the Wharton School at the University of Pennsylvania, and work experience at Fidelity and JP Morgan. She has a new markets background as an entrepreneur and advisor to startups GroupPurchase and Prosper, and developed virtual world digital asset valuation and accounting principles for Deloitte. She was involved in the early stages of the Quantified Self movement, and founded DIYgenomics in 2010, an organization that pioneered the crowdsourced health research study. She is an instructor at Singularity University, an Affiliate Scholar at the Institute for Ethics and Emerging Technologies, and a contributor to the Edge's Annual Essay Question.

Colophon

The animal on the cover of *Blockchain* is a Hungarian grey bull, a breed of domestic bull once thought to have been brought into central Europe from beyond the Carpathian mountains during the 9th-century beginnings of the Hungarian conquest. It is now known only that the breed existed in great numbers by the beginning of the 15th century, when it was already being exported in large quantities to other cities in Europe.

The toughness and adaptability of the Hungarian grey breed have made its oxen valuable as draft animals for centuries. It survives well in conditions of great freedom and so is suited to grazing on ample pasture lands. It reportedly acclimates well to a wide range of climates, and Hungarian grey heifers are reputed to be less likely to experience *dystocia*, or calving difficulty.

Elimination of pastures in the late 19th and early 20th centuries represented the first in a series of threats to the Hungarian grey's existence. Farm mechanization in the same period relaxed demand for the breed's abilities as a draft animal, and attempts to upgrade the Hungarian grey by crosses with other central European cattle further reduced the number in existence. Since a 1962 count put the number of Hungarian grey bulls alive at 6, however, enlightened breeding efforts have restored the stock to a population sufficient for maintaining genetic diversity. Largely restricted to national parks in Hungary, the breed now serves as an important genetic resource.

Many of the animals on O'Reilly covers are endangered; all of them are important to the world. To learn more about how you can help, go to *animals.oreilly.com*.

The cover image is from Cassell's *Natural History*. The cover fonts are URW Typewriter and Guardian Sans. The text font is Adobe Minion Pro; the heading font is Adobe Myriad Condensed; and the code font is Dalton Maag's Ubuntu Mono.

Have it your way.

Get even more for your money.

Join the O'Reilly Community, and register the O'Reilly books you own. It's free, and you'll get:

- $4.99 ebook upgrade offer
- 40% upgrade offer on O'Reilly print books
- Membership discounts on books and events
- Free lifetime updates to ebooks and videos
- Multiple ebook formats, DRM FREE
- Participation in the O'Reilly community
- Newsletters
- Account management
- 100% Satisfaction Guarantee

Signing up is easy:

1. Go to: oreilly.com/go/register
2. Create an O'Reilly login.
3. Provide your address.
4. Register your books.

Note: English-language books only

To order books online:
oreilly.com/store

For questions about products or an order:
orders@oreilly.com

To sign up to get topic-specific email announcements and/or news about upcoming books, conferences, special offers, and new technologies:
elists@oreilly.com

For technical questions about book content:
booktech@oreilly.com

To submit new book proposals to our editors:
proposals@oreilly.com

O'Reilly books are available in multiple DRM-free ebook formats. For more information:
oreilly.com/ebooks

O'REILLY ®

CPSIA information can be obtained
at www.ICGtesting.com
Printed in the USA
LVOW06s1949080816

499506LV00038B/232/P

9 781491 920497